The Wonder of the
MIRACLES

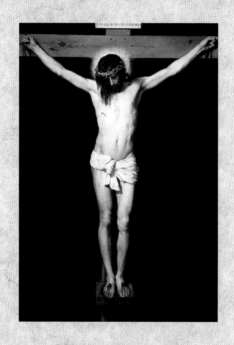

The Wonder of the
MIRACLES

ROBIN LANGLEY SOMMER

Saraband

Page 1: The Crucifixion, *a moving depiction by Velazquez.*

Page 2: *The enthroned Virgin, or* Regina Coeli *(Queen of Heaven), and Christ Child, by Raphael.*

Page 3: *The Madonna and Child, stained glass window detail.*

Published by Saraband (Scotland) Limited,
The Arthouse, 752–756 Argyle Street,
Glasgow G3 8UJ, Scotland
hermes@saraband.net

Copyright © 2004 Saraband (Scotland) Ltd.

ISBN: 1-887354-40-9

Printed in China

10 9 8 7 6 5 4 3 2

Acknowledgements
Extracts from the Authorized Version of the Bible (The King James Bible), the rights in which are vested in the Crown, are reproduced by permission of the Crown's Patentee, Cambridge University Press.

The publisher would like to thank the following people for their assistance in the preparation of this book: Clare Haworth-Maden, Debbie Hayes, Sara Hunt, Phoebe Wong, Nicola Gillies, and Wendy J. Ciaccia Eurell. Grateful acknowledgement is also made for the illustrations featured in this book, which are reproduced by courtesy of Planet Art, 2002 Arttoday.com, Inc., and CorelDraw, except those on pages 43, 47, 49, 58, 60, 61, 62 and 63, which are courtesy of Saraband Image Library.

*This book is dedicated to the memory of
the Reverend Canon Leonard A. Cragg
and to Jill Cragg, with much love.*

CONTENTS

INTRODUCTION

Miracles are defined simply as extraordinary events that surpass natural or rational explanation and thus inspire awe and wonder; depending on one's personal beliefs, they are often ascribed to a greater—superhuman—power. The miracles of the Judeo–Christian Scriptures are sometimes perceived as divine interventions that became a closed book with the fullness of Revelation. In this view, miracles of revelation, prophecy, dominion over the forces of nature, healing, even resurrection, may be interpreted primarily as proofs of God's power, rather than of His love for humankind. But just as the New Testament speaks of a new kind of human relationship with God vis-à-vis the Old Testament, so the centuries since Christ have brought increased growth in spiritual maturity, not only to professed Christians, but to all people. Whether one attributes this to the Holy Spirit, a higher power, divine unity, or the will of Allah is less significant than the fact that humankind is evolving spiritually, as well as physically, in keeping with our destiny to grow and, in Judeo–Christian belief, to become more and more fully "the image and likeness of God."

Although this book limits itself to the miracles of Jesus, as recounted in the New Testament, they may be seen as signs of love and a source of hope for all people. Other sacred scriptures tell their own stories of fellowship with God. Christ Himself said that He came for all humankind, and efforts to make God exclusive rather than inclusive have ended as mockeries of true religion. But where there is goodwill, there is grace, bringing that capacity "to wonder at" (from the Latin *mirari*) that is the essence of hopefulness, growth, and serenity, even in adversity and loss. From this perspective, we may find that most miracles come quietly and at need. The miracles recorded here still speak to anyone who has experienced illness, uncertainty, injustice, fear, or the loss of a loved one. They reassure us that we are not alone in a hostile universe, and that there is a spiritual purpose for our lives, unfolding day by day.

MIRACLES OF REVELATION

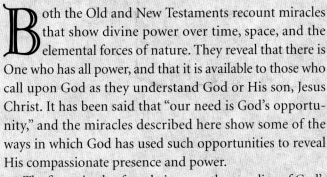

MIRACLES OF REVELATION

Previous page: Detail from a painting by Hieronymus Bosch depicting the miraculous transformation of water into wine.

Both the Old and New Testaments recount miracles that show divine power over time, space, and the elemental forces of nature. They reveal that there is One who has all power, and that it is available to those who call upon God as they understand God or His son, Jesus Christ. It has been said that "our need is God's opportunity," and the miracles described here show some of the ways in which God has used such opportunities to reveal His compassionate presence and power.

The first miracle of revelation—or the revealing of God's power—recorded by the Bible is the creation of the world. In calling forth being from nothingness, God revealed Himself as the author of life and manifested His will to share His life with others. John recounts that Jesus' first miracle of revelation occurred at the wedding in Cana, when He turned water into wine "and manifested forth his glory," causing His disciples to have faith in him.

The theme of faith is renewed in the story of Christ's calming of the storm on the Sea of Galilee (actually a large lake surrounded by hills). Mark's account tells us that "there were also with him other little ships"—probably fishing boats like those of the disciples. While Christ was sleeping in the stern of the boat, His friends were frightened by one of those storms that still blow up suddenly on the lake. High winds and waves threatened to swamp them. Finally, they awakened Christ (was He really asleep?) and urged Him to save them. Immediately, He calmed the storm with a word of command, then asked His followers, "Why are ye so fearful?

Below: By making wine take the place of water at the wedding feast, Christ revealed Himself as more than merely mortal.

how is it that ye have no faith?" They were abashed and awed by His authority over the forces of nature. The faith of Peter and the other disciples was tested again when Christ walked on water, causing those who witnessed this miraculous feat to marvel, "Of a truth thou art the Son of God." These experiences gave them a deeper insight into Christ's identity as one chosen and uniquely empowered by God.

Above: After crucifixion, Christ revealed Himself for the third time to His disciples by the sea of Tiberias, as depicted here.

The miracle of the loaves and fishes is recounted in all four Gospels, with some variation in the numbers of people fed—between four and five thousand. Described as "a multitude," they had been listening to Christ's teachings for three days, and He did not want to send them away hungry "lest they faint in the way." No one could say how it happened, but once Christ had blessed the scant supply of food on hand—some half-dozen loaves of bread and several fish—His disciples distributed it to the crowd, and everyone was fed. In fact, there were baskets of food left over when each person had eaten.

The miracle of the multiplication of the loaves and the fishes is echoed by the two miracles of the draught of fishes, the first of which revealed Christ's holiness, prompting Simon Peter to beg Him to "Depart from me; for I am a sinful man, O Lord." This miracle convinced the fishermen Simon Peter, James, and John to abandon their livelihood and instead become "fishers of men." The second miracle of the catch of fishes, which Christ performed after his Resurrection, was the third occasion on which He revealed to His disciples that "he was risen from the dead," thereby strengthening their faith and giving them hope that they, too, would enjoy life after death. "Go ye into all the world, and preach the gospel to every creature. He that believeth and is baptized shall be saved" (Mark 16:15–16).

JESUS TURNS WATER INTO WINE

Opposite: This magnificent work by Hieronymus Bosch shows a servant (detail, page 7) pouring the "good wine" at the marriage feast at Cana. This was the first of Christ's miracles.

1   And the third day there was a marriage in Cana of Galilee; and the mother of Jesus was there:

2   And both Jesus was called, and his disciples, to the marriage.

3   And when they wanted wine, the mother of Jesus saith unto him, They have no wine.

4   Jesus saith unto her, Woman, what have I to do with thee? mine hour is not yet come.

5   His mother saith unto the servants, Whatsoever he saith unto you, do *it*.

6   And there were set there six waterpots of stone, after the manner of the purifying of the Jews, containing two or three firkins apiece.

7   Jesus saith unto them, Fill the waterpots with water. And they filled them up to the brim.

8   And he saith unto them, Draw out now, and bear unto the governor of the feast. And they bare *it*.

9   When the ruler of the feast had tasted the water that was made wine, and knew not whence it was: (but the servants which drew the water knew;) the governor of the feast called the bridegroom,

10   And saith unto him, Every man at the beginning doth set forth good wine; and when men have well drunk, then that which is worse: *but* thou hast kept the good wine until now.

11   This beginning of miracles did Jesus in Cana of Galilee, and manifested forth his glory; and his disciples believed on him.

—JOHN 2:1–11

JESUS CALMS THE STORM

Opposite: An evocative painting of turbulent seas, by Claude Monet.

36 And when they had sent away the multitude, they took him even as he was in the ship. And there were also with him other little ships.

37 And there arose a great storm of wind, and the waves beat into the ship, so that it was now full.

38 And he was in the hinder part of the ship, asleep on a pillow: and they awake him, and say unto him, Master, carest thou not that we perish?

39 And he arose, and rebuked the wind, and said unto the sea, Peace, be still. And the wind ceased, and there was a great calm.

40 And he said unto them, Why are ye so fearful? how is it that ye have no faith?

41 And they feared exceedingly, and said one to another, What manner of man is this, that even the wind and the sea obey him?

—MARK 4:36–41

Right: The frightened apostles awaken Jesus to save them from the sudden storm on the Sea of Galilee. His command quiets wind and wave, to the wonder of his followers.

JESUS WALKS ON WATER

22 And straightway Jesus constrained his disciples to get into a ship, and to go before him unto the other side, while he sent the multitudes away.

23 And when he had sent the multitudes away, he went up into a mountain apart to pray: and when the evening was come, he was there alone.

24 But the ship was now in the midst of the sea, tossed with waves: for the wind was contrary.

25 And in the fourth watch of the night Jesus went unto them, walking on the sea.

26 And when the disciples saw him walking on the sea, they were troubled, saying, It is a spirit; and they cried out for fear.

27 But straightway Jesus spake unto them, saying, Be of good cheer; it is I; be not afraid.

28 And Peter answered him and said, Lord, if it be thou, bid me come unto thee on the water.

29 And he said, Come. And when Peter was come down out of the ship, he walked on the water, to go to Jesus.

30 But when he saw the wind boisterous, he was afraid; and beginning to sink, he cried, saying, Lord, save me.

31 And immediately Jesus stretched forth *his* hand, and caught him, and said unto him, O thou of little faith, wherefore didst thou doubt?

32 And when they were come into the ship, the wind ceased.

33 Then they that were in the ship came and worshipped him, saying, Of a truth thou art the Son of God.

—MATTHEW 14:22–33

Opposite: *Much to the disciples' amazement, "Jesus went unto them, walking on the sea" (Matthew 14:25).*

THE LOAVES AND THE FISHES MULTIPLIED

32 Then Jesus called his disciples *unto him*, and said, I have compassion on the multitude, because they continue with me now three days, and have nothing to eat: and I will not send them away fasting, lest they faint in the way.

33 And his disciples say unto him, Whence should we have so much bread in the wilderness, as to fill so great a multitude?

34 And Jesus saith unto them, How many loaves have ye? And they said, Seven, and a few little fishes.

35 And he commanded the multitude to sit down on the ground.

36 And he took the seven loaves and the fishes, and gave thanks, and brake *them*, and gave to his disciples, and the disciples to the multitude.

37 And they did all eat, and were filled: and they took up of the broken *meat* that was left seven baskets full.

38 And they that did eat were four thousand men, beside women and children.

—MATTHEW 15:32–38

Opposite and right:
Jesus fed a crowd of thousands, with enough to spare, even though their supplies had been limited to only a handful of loaves and fishes.

Left: *Raphael's beautiful painting depicts the disciples pulling in their nets, burdened with a "great multitude of fishes" (Luke 5:6), where earlier they had found none. The painting was a cartoon for a tapestry, created early in the sixteenth century.*

A MULTITUDE OF FISHES

1 And it came to pass, that, as the people pressed upon him to hear the word of God, he stood by the lake of Gennesaret,

2 And saw two ships standing by the lake: but the fishermen were gone out of them, and were washing *their* nets.

3 And he entered into one of the ships, which was Simon's, and prayed him that he would thrust out a little from the land. And he sat down, and taught the people out of the ship.

4 Now when he had left speaking, he said unto Simon, Launch out into the deep, and let down your nets for a draught.

5 And Simon answering said unto him, Master, we have toiled all the night, and have taken nothing: nevertheless at thy word I will let down the net.

6 And when they had this done, they inclosed a great multitude of fishes: and their net brake.

7 And they beckoned unto *their* partners, which were in the other ship, that they should come and help them. And they came, and filled both the ships, so that they began to sink.

8 When Simon Peter saw *it*, he fell down at Jesus' knees, saying, Depart from me; for I am a sinful man, O Lord.

9 For he was astonished, and all that were with him, at the draught of the fishes which they had taken:

10 And so *was* also James, and John, the sons of Zebedee, which were partners with Simon. And Jesus said unto Simon, Fear not; from henceforth thou shalt catch men.

11 And when they had brought their ships to land, they forsook all, and followed him.

—LUKE 5:1–11

THE RESURRECTED CHRIST FEEDS THE DISCIPLES

1 After these things Jesus shewed himself again to the disciples at the sea of Tiberias; and on this wise shewed he *himself.*

2 There were together Simon Peter, and Thomas called Didymus, and Nathanael of Cana in Galilee, and the *sons* of Zebedee, and two other of his disciples.

3 Simon Peter saith unto them, I go a fishing. They say unto him, We also go with thee. They went forth, and

Below and overleaf:
Jesus appeared before His disciples while they dined at Emmaus (overleaf, as portrayed by Titian).

entered into a ship immediately; and that night they caught nothing.

4   But when the morning was now come, Jesus stood on the shore: but the disciples knew not that it was Jesus.

5   Then Jesus saith unto them, Children, have ye any meat? They answered him, No.

6   And he said unto them, Cast the net on the right side of the ship, and ye shall find. They cast therefore, and now they were not able to draw it for the multitude of fishes.

7   Therefore that disciple whom Jesus loved saith unto Peter, It is the Lord. Now when Simon Peter heard that it was the Lord, he girt *his* fisher's coat *unto him,* (for he was naked,) and did cast himself into the sea.

8   And the other disciples came in a little ship; (for they were not far from land, but as it were two hundred cubits,) dragging the net with fishes.

9   As soon then as they were come to land, they saw a fire of coals there, and fish laid thereon, and bread.

10 Jesus saith unto them, Bring of the fish which ye have now caught.

11 Simon Peter went up, and drew the net to land full of great fishes, an hundred and fifty and three: and for all there were so many, yet was not the net broken.

12 Jesus saith unto them, Come *and* dine. And none of the disciples durst ask him, Who art thou? knowing that it was the Lord.

13 Jesus then cometh, and taketh bread, and giveth them, and fish likewise.

14 This is now the third time that Jesus shewed himself to his disciples, after that he was risen from the dead.

—JOHN 21:1–14

MIRACLES OF
PROPHECY

MIRACLES OF PROPHECY

Previous page: Fra Angelico's luminous depiction of the Annunciation (1441).

Opposite: The prophet Isaiah, painted by Michelangelo with heavy-lidded eyes and brow furrowed in thought, closes his book as his attendant cherub points to the Sistine Chapel fresco of the Fall of Man.

Prophecy can be defined not only as the foretelling of future events, but as the living-out of a destiny or example in one's own time and place. Martin Luther King, Jr., for instance, is widely considered a modern-day prophet for his role in the American civil rights movement. He stirred the conscience of a nation by his courageous, nonviolent resistance to racism and prophesied his own death by assassination only days before he was killed. In so doing, he became one of a long line of men and women who answered a call that took precedence over everything else in their lives, thus becoming both the messenger and the message.

In the Book of Isaiah, we find miraculous prophecies of the Christ ("Anointed One") to come, even to His rejection by His own people and the manner of His Passion and death. These "suffering servant" prophecies of Isaiah must have been deeply mysterious to his contemporaries, who expected a Messiah whose reign would be as materially splendid as that of King Solomon, or of Christ's ancestor, David. Humility and obscurity were not the qualities that they looked for in a king. Not even Christ's disciples understood the terms upon which He had come into the world until after the Resurrection. The passage from Isaiah included here is well known as an oratorio from the beautiful score of Handel's *Messiah*: "Surely he hath borne our griefs and carried our sorrows."

One of the scenes most often depicted in Christian sacred art is that of the angel Gabriel coming to the Virgin Mary to tell her that she has been chosen to become the mother of the Messiah. This miracle of prophecy was the culmination of all those that had preceded it in the Old Testament, from the promise of a redeemer to Adam to the announcement to Micah that Bethlehem would be the Messiah's birthplace. Mary was espoused to Joseph of Nazareth, a descendant of the family of David, but they had not yet lived together, so she asked the angelic messenger: "How shall this be seeing I know not a man?" He told her that the child to come would

be born of the Holy Spirit, "therefore also that holy thing which shall be born of thee shall be called the Son of God." This news of the Incarnation far exceeded the hopes and expectations of Israel. But Mary assented to this profound mystery, assured that "with God nothing shall be impossible."

The moving star that led the wise men from the East (probably Babylon) to Bethlehem was a sign that the Gentiles, as well as the Jews, were to be ruled by the newborn king of Israel. This prophecy had recurred throughout the Old Testament, as in the Book of Malachi, but was not clearly understood. The Israelites were focused on the promises made to them as a people chosen by God. Thus King Herod was shocked and dismayed, "and all Jerusalem with him," when the wise men appeared in the city seeking "he that is born King of the Jews," so that they might worship him. Directed to Bethlehem by Herod, who had already formed a plan to kill the child as a rival, they followed the star "til it came and stood over where the young child was." Rejoicing, they offered the symbolic gifts of gold, frankincense, and myrrh, signifying kingship, deity, and entombment. It is significant that "they departed into their own country another way" after being warned in a dream not to return to Herod. Having been called to prophesy and to worship the Messiah, they were profoundly changed and would never be as they had been before.

Christ's cousin John, called the Baptist, was the prophet who announced the Messiah to His own generation. Although they grew up together, it appears that John became fully aware that Christ was the promised redeemer only when He came to him for baptism in the River Jordan. John was reluctant to administer the baptism of repentance because he discerned that Christ was totally free of sin. But Christ persuaded him that it must be done to set an example and to confirm His mission to Israel. When He emerged from the river, a voice from heaven announced: "This is my beloved Son, in whom I am well pleased." Thus John the Baptist fulfilled his prophetic role as "the voice of one crying in the wilderness, 'Prepare ye the way of the Lord.'"

Opposite: The Adoration of the Magi, *a stunning painting by Hieronymus Bosch that forms the center panel of a triptych. Christ's coming had been foretold in the Old Testament.*

ISAIAH ON CHRIST'S PASSION

1   Who hath believed our report? and to whom is the arm of the LORD revealed?

2   For he shall grow up before him as a tender plant, and as a root out of a dry ground: he hath no form nor comeliness; and when we shall see him, *there is* no beauty that we should desire him.

3   He is despised and rejected of men; a man of sorrows, and acquainted with grief: and we hid as it were *our* faces from him; he was despised, and we esteemed him not.

4   Surely he hath borne our griefs, and carried our sorrows: yet we did esteem him stricken, smitten of God, and afflicted.

5   But he *was* wounded for our transgressions, *he was* bruised for our iniquities: the chastisement of our peace *was* upon him; and with his stripes we are healed.

6   All we like sheep have gone astray; we have turned every one to his own way; and the LORD hath laid on him the iniquity of us all.

7   He was oppressed, and he was afflicted, yet he opened not his mouth: he is brought as a lamb to the slaughter, and as a sheep before her shearers is dumb, so he openeth not his mouth.

8   He was taken from prison and from judgment: and who shall declare his generation? for he was cut off out of the land of the living: for the transgression of my people was he stricken.

—ISAIAH 53:1–8

Opposite: *Fra Angelico's panel (c. 1450–55) shows Christ on the cross with the Virgin, St. John the Evangelist, and a Dominican cardinal.*

Below: *The preeminent prophet of the Messiah, Isaiah foretold the manner of Christ's birth and of his death, seen here in Raphael's masterwork* The Entombment *(1507).*

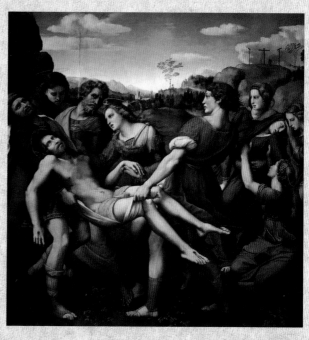

THE ANNUNCIATION

26 And in the sixth month the angel Gabriel was sent from God unto a city of Galilee, named Nazareth,

27 To a virgin espoused to a man whose name was Joseph, of the house of David; and the virgin's name *was* Mary.

28 And the angel came in unto her, and said, Hail, *thou that art* highly favoured, the Lord *is* with thee: blessed *art* thou among women.

29 And when she saw *him*, she was troubled at his saying, and cast in her mind what manner of salutation this should be.

Right: Fra Angelico painted the Annunciation several times, but this panel (c. 1432–33) is his first depiction of the scene. It is widely considered his first great artistic masterpiece.

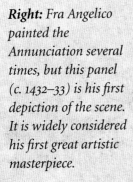

30 And the angel said unto her, Fear not, Mary: for thou hast found favour with God.

31 And, behold, thou shalt conceive in thy womb, and bring forth a son, and shalt call his name JESUS.

32 He shall be great, and shall be called the Son of the Highest: and the Lord God shall give unto him the throne of his father David:

33 And he shall reign over the house of Jacob for ever; and of his kingdom there shall be no end.

34 Then said Mary unto the angel, How shall this be, seeing I know not a man?

35 And the angel answered and said unto her, The Holy Ghost shall come upon thee, and the power of the Highest shall overshadow

thee: therefore also that holy thing which shall be born of thee shall be called the Son of God.

36 And, behold, thy cousin Elisabeth, she hath also conceived a son in her old age: and this is the sixth month with her, who was called barren.

37 For with God nothing shall be impossible.

38 And Mary said, Behold the handmaid of the Lord; be it unto me according to thy word. And the angel departed from her.

—LUKE 1:26–38

Left: In Botticelli's widely admired painting of the Annunciation (1489–90), the angel holds a white lily, which symbolizes the Virgin's purity.

THE STAR OF BETHLEHEM

1   Now when Jesus was born in Bethlehem of Judaea in the days of Herod the king, behold, there came wise men from the east to Jerusalem,

2   Saying, Where is he that is born King of the Jews? for we have seen his star in the east, and are come to worship him.

3   When Herod the king had heard *these things*, he was troubled, and all Jerusalem with him.

4   And when he had gathered all the chief priests and scribes of the people together, he demanded of them where Christ should be born.

5   And they said unto him, In Bethlehem of Judaea: for thus it is written by the prophet,

6   And thou Bethlehem, *in* the land of Juda, art not the least among the princes of Juda: for out of thee shall come a Governor, that shall rule my people Israel.

7   Then Herod, when he had privily called the wise men, inquired of them diligently what time the star appeared.

8   And he sent them to Bethlehem, and said, Go and search diligently for the young child; and when ye have found *him*, bring me word again, that I may come and worship him also.

9   When they had heard the king, they departed; and, lo, the star, which they saw in the east, went before them, till it came and stood over where the young child was.

Right: *This detail of a panel by Hieronymus Bosch shows the Magi presenting their gifts to the newborn Christ, whom they had found by following the Star of Bethlehem.*

10 When they saw the star, they rejoiced with exceeding great joy.

11 And when they were come into the house, they saw the young child with Mary his mother, and fell down, and worshipped him: and when they had opened their treasures, they presented unto him gifts; gold, and frankincense, and myrrh.

12 And being warned of God in a dream that they should not return to Herod, they departed into their own country another way.

—MATTHEW 2:1–12

THE BAPTISM OF CHRIST

1 In those days came John the Baptist, preaching in the wilderness of Judaea,

2 And saying, Repent ye: for the kingdom of heaven is at hand.

3 For this is he that was spoken of by the prophet Esaias, saying, The voice of one crying in the wilderness, Prepare ye the way of the Lord, make his paths straight.

4 And the same John had his raiment of camel's hair, and a leathern girdle about his loins; and his meat was locusts and wild honey.

5 Then went out to him Jerusalem, and all Judaea, and all the region round about Jordan,

6 And were baptized of him in Jordan, confessing their sins.

7 But when he saw many of the Pharisees and Sadducees come to his baptism, he said unto them, O generation of vipers, who hath warned you to flee from the wrath to come?

8 Bring forth therefore fruits meet for repentance:

9 And think not to say within yourselves, We have Abraham to *our* father: for I say unto you, that God is able of these stones to raise up children unto Abraham.

10 And now also the axe is laid unto the root of the trees: therefore every tree which bringeth not forth good fruit is hewn down, and cast into the fire.

11 I indeed baptize you with water unto repentance: but he that cometh after me is mightier than I, whose shoes I am not worthy to bear: he shall baptize you with the Holy Ghost, and *with* fire.

—MATTHEW 3:1–11

Opposite page: Christ receives baptism from His cousin John, His identity confirmed by the Holy Spirit above His head, as depicted by Andrea del Verrocchio (1470). Leonardo da Vinci painted one of the angels shown at left when he was a young student under Verrocchio's tutelage.

Overleaf: The Adoration of the Child, by Hieronymus Bosch.

MIRACLES OF
FORGIVENESS

MIRACLES OF FORGIVENESS

Previous page: *Mary Magdalene, the sister of Lazarus and Martha, surrenders herself to God after Christ forgives her sins. The skull appears as the attribute of a penitent saint in this painting by Titian.*

Below: *Instead of condemning and judging people for their sins, Christ set an example by forgiving. Here he is seen with the adulteress, whom he saved from death by stoning.*

All of the miracles of forgiveness described here are highly personal. They show the unique relationship between God and each person, and the mysterious ways in which grace flows from one to another.

The well-known story of the woman taken in adultery shows Christ's transcendence of the Old Law: mercy takes precedence over traditional concepts of justice. Of course, the Ten Commandments, while prohibiting adultery, did not stipulate that it should be punished by stoning to death. This law was the product of a patriarchal society with rigid strictures around bloodlines and inheritance. (There was no provision for stoning male adulterers.) The scribes and Pharisees who brought the accused woman to Christ for judgment were "convicted by their own conscience" when He challenged them: "He that is without sin among you, let him first cast a stone at her." This profound statement was the basis for a new spiritual principle that encouraged humility and self-examination instead of rash judgment and condemnation. It was underlined by Christ's words to the frightened woman after her accusers had drifted away: "Has anyone condemned you? ... Neither do I condemn you."

At the healing pool of Bethesda in Jerusalem, all of the people with infirmities who hoped for a cure are described as "impotent," that is, powerless. The man whom Christ addresses has been unable to walk for thirty-eight years—nearly a lifetime in the New Testament era. It is significant that Christ does not ask him whether he wants to walk, but whether he wants to get well. It seems that Christ had dis-

cerned a problem deeper than that of physical paralysis: perhaps a fear of taking on
the responsibility that comes with being
empowered rather than impotent. This
idea is borne out by Christ's words to the
newly healed man when He meets him later
in the Temple: "Behold, thou art made
whole; sin no more lest a worse thing come
unto thee."

People of every faith and condition have
been inspired by Christ's compassionate
words from the cross: "Father, forgive them;
for they know not what they do." In the
face of hatred, torture, and imminent death,
He reiterated His message of love and reconciliation between God and humankind.
Devout Christians have said that a single
drop of Christ's blood would have been
sufficient to atone for every sin ever committed, but He
chose freely to pour out His entire life to show the infinite
depths of divine love and forgiveness. When the veil of the
Temple was "rent in two from top to bottom" at the moment
of His death, it was not to signify blasphemy according to
Jewish law, but to show that the holiest of sanctuaries had
been opened to all by Christ's self-sacrifice.

*Above: When Christ
had endured extremes
of humiliation and
agony, he still pleaded
to God from the cross:
"Father, forgive them,
for they know not what
they do."*

Shortly after His Resurrection, Christ showed that He
forgave Peter for his threefold denial that he knew Christ
and was one of His disciples. Driven by fear, Peter had dis-
sociated himself from Christ after His arrest, and had then
gone out and "wept bitterly." In this post-Resurrection
appearance, Christ showed that He had already forgiven
Peter and gave him the chance to forgive himself. He asked
Peter three times, "Do you love me?" so that his previous
denials would be wiped out by his reaffirmation of love and
loyalty. Thus Peter was renewed and strengthened for his
leadership role in spreading the gospel ("good news"), and
Christ commanded him to: "Feed my lambs; feed my sheep."

⁓ THE WONDER OF THE MIRACLES

Opposite: St. Peter, detail, by Masaccio.

Below: The penitent St. Peter is endowed by the Risen Christ with "the keys of the Kingdom" in this Renaissance painting by Perugino (1481).

St. Paul's experience on the road to Damascus is a powerful example of simultaneous forgiveness and conversion. A zealous persecutor of the followers of Christ, whose Hebrew name was Saul ("asked for"), Paul was literally knocked from his horse and stricken with blindness so that he could be forgiven and set upon a new course. Because Paul was receptive to the message that he received through divine intervention, all of his energy and abilities were rechanneled into his new ministry as a profound influence for good upon the early Christian community.

THE WOMAN TAKEN IN ADULTERY

Opposite: The woman taken in adultery is saved from death by stoning through the compassionate intervention of Christ, who bade her accusers to look into their own consciences.

2 And early in the morning he came again into the temple, and all the people came unto him; and he sat down, and taught them.

3 And the scribes and Pharisees brought unto him a woman taken in adultery; and when they had set her in the midst,

4 They say unto him, Master, this woman was taken in adultery, in the very act.

5 Now Moses in the law commanded us, that such should be stoned: but what sayest thou?

6 This they said, tempting him, that they might have to accuse him. But Jesus stooped down, and with *his* finger wrote on the ground, *as though he heard them not.*

7 So when they continued asking him, he lifted up himself, and said unto them, He that is without sin among you, let him first cast a stone at her.

8 And again he stooped down, and wrote on the ground.

9 And they which heard *it*, being convicted by *their own* conscience, went out one by one, beginning at the eldest, *even* unto the last: and Jesus was left alone, and the woman standing in the midst.

10 When Jesus had lifted up himself, and saw none but the woman, he said unto her, Woman, where are those thine accusers? hath no man condemned thee?

11 She said, No man, Lord. And Jesus said unto her, Neither do I condemn thee: go, and sin no more.

—JOHN 8:2–11

THE SICK MAN AT BETHESDA

2   Now there is at Jerusalem by the sheep market a pool, which is called in the Hebrew tongue Bethesda, having five porches.

3   In these lay a great multitude of impotent folk, of blind, halt, withered, waiting for the moving of the water.

4   For an angel went down at a certain season into the pool, and troubled the water: whosoever then first after the troubling of the water stepped in was made whole of whatsoever disease he had.

Below: At Bethesda, Jesus healed a man who had spent most of his life unable to walk.

Left: *The healed man was later told: "Sin no more lest a worse thing come unto thee" (John 5:14).*

5 And a certain man was there, which had an infirmity thirty and eight years.

6 When Jesus saw him lie, and knew that he had been now a long time in that case, he saith unto him, Wilt thou be made whole?

7 The impotent man answered him, Sir, I have no man, when the water is troubled, to put me into the pool: but while I am coming, another steppeth down before me.

8 Jesus saith unto him, Rise, take up thy bed, and walk.

9 And immediately the man was made whole, and took up his bed, and walked: and on the same day was the sabbath.

10 The Jews therefore said unto him that was cured, It is the sabbath day: it is not lawful for thee to carry *thy* bed.

11 He answered them, He that made me whole, the same said unto me, Take up thy bed, and walk.

12 Then asked they him, What man is that which said unto thee, Take up thy bed, and walk?

13 And he that was healed wist not who it was: for Jesus had conveyed himself away, a multitude being in *that* place.

14 Afterward Jesus findeth him in the temple, and said unto him, Behold, thou art made whole: sin no more, lest a worse thing come unto thee.

15 The man departed, and told the Jews that it was Jesus, which had made him whole.

—JOHN 5:2–15

CHRIST FORGIVES HIS EXECUTIONERS

Opposite: The crucified Christ (depicted here by Raphael) speaks words of forgiveness to his executioners. "Father, forgive them," He prayed, "for they know not what they do" (Luke 23:34).

23 And they were instant with loud voices, requiring that he might be crucified. And the voices of them and of the chief priests prevailed.

24 And Pilate gave sentence that it should be as they required.

25 And he released unto them him that for sedition and murder was cast into prison, whom they had desired; but he delivered Jesus to their will.

26 And as they led him away, they laid hold upon one Simon, a Cyrenian, coming out of the country, and on him they laid the cross, that he might bear *it* after Jesus.

27 And there followed him a great company of people, and of women, which also bewailed and lamented him.

28 But Jesus turning unto them said, Daughters of Jerusalem, weep not for me, but weep for yourselves, and for your children.

29 For, behold, the days are coming, in the which they shall say, Blessed *are* the barren, and the wombs that never bare, and the paps which never gave suck.

30 Then shall they begin to say to the mountains, Fall on us; and to the hills, Cover us.

31 For if they do these things in a green tree, what shall be done in the dry?

32 And there were also two other, malefactors, led with him to be put to death.

33 And when they were come to the place, which is called Calvary, there they crucified him, and the malefactors, one on the right hand, and the other on the left.

34 Then said Jesus, Father, forgive them; for they know not what they do. And they parted his raiment, and cast lots.

—LUKE 23:23–34

THE CONVERSION OF ST. PAUL

Opposite: "There shined round about him a light from heaven" (Acts 9:3).

Below: Blinded by the light of Christ, St. Paul is supported by a fellow traveler on the road to Damascus, where he had planned to imprison Jewish converts to Christianity.

1 And Saul, yet breathing out threatenings and slaughter against the disciples of the Lord, went unto the high priest,

2 And desired of him letters to Damascus to the synagogues, that if he found any of this way, whether they were men or women, he might bring them bound unto Jerusalem.

3 And as he journeyed, he came near Damascus: and suddenly there shined round about him a light from heaven:

4 And he fell to the earth, and heard a voice saying unto him, Saul, Saul, why persecutest thou me?

5 And he said, Who art thou, Lord? And the Lord said, I am Jesus whom thou persecutest: *it is* hard for thee to kick against the pricks.

6 And he trembling and astonished said, Lord, what wilt thou have me to do? And the Lord *said* unto him, Arise, and go into the city, and it shall be told thee what thou must do.

—ACTS 9:1–6

PETER FORGIVEN FOR HIS DENIAL OF CHRIST

Below: An angel appears to free Peter from prison after his arrest for preaching the Risen Christ as the savior of the world. Raphael painted this striking image during the Italian Renaissance.

14 This is now the third time that Jesus shewed himself to his disciples, after that he was risen from the dead.

15 So when they had dined, Jesus saith to Simon Peter, Simon, *son* of Jonas, lovest thou me more than these? He saith unto him, Yea, Lord; thou knowest that I love thee. He saith unto him, Feed my lambs.

16 He saith to him again the second time, Simon, *son* of Jonas, lovest thou me? He saith unto him, Yea, Lord; thou knowest that I love thee. He saith unto him, Feed my sheep.

17 He saith unto him the third time, Simon, *son* of Jonas, lovest thou me? Peter was grieved because he said unto him the third time, Lovest thou me? And he said unto him, Lord, thou knowest all things; thou knowest that I love thee. Jesus saith unto him, Feed my sheep.

18 Verily, verily, I say unto thee, When thou wast young, thou girdedst thyself, and walkedst whither thou wouldest: but when thou shalt be old, thou shalt stretch forth thy hands, and another shall gird thee, and carry *thee* whither thou wouldest not.

19 This spake he, signifying by what death he should glorify God. And when he had spoken this, he saith unto him, Follow me.

—JOHN 21:14–19

MIRACLES OF
HEALING

Miracles of Healing

Previous page: *Jesus'
earthly role was to
protect and heal his
"flock," and He is
often portrayed with
a symbolic lamb, as
in this painting by
Leonardo da Vinci.*

Opposite: *His wounds
healed and glorified by
His resurrection, Christ
appears to His mother
Mary before His
wondering disciples
and a company of
angels in Titian's
portrait of 1554.*

In the whole of the New Testament, there is no record of Christ's refusing a sincere request for healing. The stories of the ten lepers who were cleansed, of blind Bartimaeus, of the man with a withered hand, and of many others, show the universal compassion and power of God as personified in Christ.

Several common threads run through the seven miracles of healing described here. First, those who asked for Christ's intervention were willing to believe that He could help them and that He wanted to do so. Second, all who approached Him had been disempowered in some way by their afflictions, which prevented them from experiencing life in its fullness. And in many of these healings, Christ furthermore not only revealed Himself, but put Himself at risk.

The powerful Pharisees, who upheld the rigid strictures of the Mosaic law, opposed Christ for healing on the Sabbath and sparing the life of a woman taken in adultery. They accused Him of blasphemy when He assured a man disabled by palsy that his sins were forgiven. In fact, they were jealous of His influence and alarmed by the new teachings of God's universal love and mercy, which threatened their status. In revealing Himself, Christ faced the risk that we all do: that of rejection and hostility. In taking on our humanity, He took on our vulnerability. We see this in the question He asked one of the ten lepers—the only one who returned to thank Him: "Were there not ten cleansed? but where are the nine?" His feelings were involved, but His primary concern was that God should be glorified by the miracle, and that the person who had experienced it should be healed at every level. Thus He says in this case, as in so many others: "Arise, go thy way: thy faith hath made thee whole."

In the case of the woman with a hemorrhage, the petitioner approached Him secretly, telling herself, "If I may but touch his garment, I shall be whole." Her faith and humility were revealed and commended to all. Christ was

Above: Christ's power to restore sight to the blind signified the new light that had come into the world.

also moved by the compassion of those who sought healing on another's behalf, like the centurion who asked for his servant's recovery. A Roman military official, he had already shown goodwill in building a synagogue for the people. In coming to Christ, he put aside his privileges to seek help from the citizen of an occupied country. His faith, too, was honored and held up as an example to the Jews, who sought to retain their identity as a chosen people at the expense of "the Gentiles"— that is, all others.

The universality of Christ's healing and saving mission is seen in the miracle whereby He delivered the daughter of a Greek (Gentile) woman from "an unclean spirit." Hearing of Christ's presence in the vicinity of Tyre and Sidon, the woman came to his lodging (where, Mark tells us, "he could not be hid") and begged Him to free her child of possession. Christ tested her faith by telling her that the children of Israel had the first claim upon Him, but she would not be discouraged from her appeal, even comparing herself to a dog that might eat of the crumbs that fell from the children's table. Deeply moved by this show of humility and trust, Christ sent her home with the promise: "the devil [adversary] is gone out of thy daughter."

Many people have interpreted Biblical accounts of demonic possession as references to epilepsy and similar seizure disorders, or to psychosis. Others see them as literal accounts of exorcism. Whatever the case, the afflicted person is controlled by some force inimical to his or her life, which Christ overcomes. Another story of healing and deliverance is set in the synagogue at Capernaum, where the man who addresses Christ appears to be controlled by an evil entity (described as "a spirit of an unclean devil") that shows fear in Christ's presence. "Let us alone," it demands. "What have we to do with thee, thou Jesus of Nazareth? art thou come to destroy us? I know thee who thou art; the Holy One of God." Jesus rebukes the unseen power and commands it to leave the man. "And when the devil had thrown him in the midst, he came out of him, and hurt him not."

Below: A Doré engraving of Christ in the Temple, where he performed many miracles of healing and taught His followers the deeper meaning of the Hebrew scriptures.

These miracles confront the mystery of evil and suffering in the world by showing that evil itself can be transformed into good, not only for the individual, but for the human community. Many have prayed for physical healing and have experienced it; others have received the power to accept their condition as an opportunity for spiritual growth and strengthened relationships with family and friends. Still others have made the ultimate act of faith in coming to understand that some things can only be healed by death.

Right: *The scourge of leprosy made one an outcast from the community; cleansed by Christ, the grateful leper from Samaria was the only one who returned to give thanks for his restoration to life and health.*

THE TEN LEPERS

11 And it came to pass, as he went to Jerusalem, that he passed through the midst of Samaria and Galilee.

12 And as he entered into a certain village, there met him ten men that were lepers, which stood afar off:

13 And they lifted up *their* voices, and said, Jesus, Master, have mercy on us.

14 And when he saw *them*, he said unto them, Go shew yourselves unto the priests. And it came to pass, that, as they went, they were cleansed.

15 And one of them, when he saw that he was healed, turned back, and with a loud voice glorified God,

16 And fell down on *his* face at his feet, giving him thanks: and he was a Samaritan.

17 And Jesus answering said, Were there not ten cleansed? but where *are* the nine?

18 There are not found that returned to give glory to God, save this stranger.

19 And he said unto him, Arise, go thy way: thy faith hath made thee whole.

—LUKE 17:11–19

BLIND BARTIMAEUS

46 And they came to Jericho: and as he went out of Jericho with his disciples and a great number of people, blind Bartimaeus, the son of Timaeus, sat by the highway side begging.

47 And when he heard that it was Jesus of Nazareth, he began to cry out, and say, Jesus, *thou* Son of David, have mercy on me.

48 And many charged him that he should hold his peace: but he cried the more a great deal, *Thou* Son of David, have mercy on me.

49 And Jesus stood still, and commanded him to be called. And they call the blind man, saying unto him, Be of good comfort, rise; he calleth thee.

50 And he, casting away his garment, rose, and came to Jesus.

51 And Jesus answered and said unto him, What wilt thou that I should do unto thee? The blind man said unto him, Lord, that I might receive my sight.

52 And Jesus said unto him, Go thy way; thy faith hath made thee whole. And immediately he received his sight, and followed Jesus in the way.

—MARK 10:46–52

Left: *The blind beggar Bartimaeus refused to be silenced by the crowd when he heard that Christ was passing by. He cried out repeatedly, "Jesus, thou Son of David, have mercy on me."*

THE MAN WITH A WITHERED HAND

Below: Christ heals the sick, who flock to Him as word of His wonder-working power spreads through Jerusalem and surrounding villages.

9 And when he was departed thence, he went into their synagogue:

10 And, behold, there was a man which had *his* hand withered. And they asked him, saying, Is it lawful to heal on the sabbath days? that they might accuse him.

11 And he said unto them, What man shall there be among you, that shall have one sheep, and if it fall into a pit on the sabbath day, will he not lay hold on it, and lift *it* out?

12 How much then is a man better than a sheep? Wherefore it is lawful to do well on the sabbath days.

13 Then saith he to the man, Stretch forth thine hand. And he stretched *it* forth; and it was restored whole, like as the other.

14 Then the Pharisees went out, and held a council against him, how they might destroy him.

—MATTHEW 12:9–14

THE MAN WITH PALSY

2 And, behold, they brought to him a man sick of the palsy, lying on a bed: and Jesus seeing their faith said unto the sick of the palsy; Son, be of good cheer; thy sins be forgiven thee.

3 And, behold, certain of the scribes said within themselves, This *man* blasphemeth.

4 And Jesus knowing their thoughts said, Wherefore think ye evil in your hearts?

5 For whether is easier to say, *Thy* sins be forgiven thee; or to say, Arise, and walk?

6 But that ye may know that the Son of man hath power on earth to forgive sins, (then saith he to the sick of the palsy,) Arise, take up thy bed, and go unto thine house.

7 And he arose, and departed to his house.

8 But when the multitudes saw *it*, they marvelled, and glorified God, which had given such power unto men.

—MATTHEW 9:2–8

Below: The man stricken with palsy is commanded to "Arise, take up thy bed."

THE WOMAN OF GREAT FAITH

20 And, behold, a woman, which was diseased with an issue of blood twelve years, came behind *him*, and touched the hem of his garment:

21 For she said within herself, If I may but touch his garment, I shall be whole.

22 But Jesus turned him about, and when he saw her, he said, Daughter, be of good comfort; thy faith hath made thee whole. And the woman was made whole from that hour.

—MATTHEW 9:20–22

Right: A stark portrait by Vincent van Gogh recalls the suffering of the woman who turned to Christ for relief from an illness that had afflicted her for twelve years.

THE CENTURION'S SERVANT

2   And a certain centurion's servant, who was dear unto him, was sick, and ready to die.

3   And when he heard of Jesus, he sent unto him the elders of the Jews, beseeching him that he would come and heal his servant.

4   And when they came to Jesus, they besought him instantly, saying, That he was worthy for whom he should do this:

5   For he loveth our nation, and he hath built us a synagogue.

6   Then Jesus went with them. And when he was now not far from the house, the centurion sent friends to him, saying unto him, Lord, trouble not thyself: for I am not worthy that thou shouldest enter under my roof:

7   Wherefore neither thought I myself worthy to come unto thee: but say in a word, and my servant shall be healed.

8   For I also am a man set under authority, having under me soldiers, and I say unto one, Go, and he goeth; and to another, Come, and he cometh; and to my servant, Do this, and he doeth *it*.

9   When Jesus heard these things, he marvelled at him, and turned him about, and said unto the people that followed him, I say unto you, I have not found so great faith, no, not in Israel.

10 And they that were sent, returning to the house, found the servant whole that had been sick.

—LUKE 7:2–10

Below: *Grieving parents seek Christ's intercession for their sick child in an engraving by Doré.*

THE WOMAN WHOSE DAUGHTER WAS POSSESSED

Below: Christ is moved by the pleas of the Gentile woman whose daughter is possessed, although his companions turn their backs on her in this illustration from the Middle Ages.

24 And from thence he arose, and went into the borders of Tyre and Sidon, and entered into an house, and would have no man know *it*: but he could not be hid.

25 For a *certain* woman, whose young daughter had an unclean spirit, heard of him, and came and fell at his feet:

26 The woman was a Greek, a Syrophenician by nation; and she besought him that he would cast forth the devil out of her daughter.

27 But Jesus said unto her, Let the children first be filled: for it is not meet to take the children's bread, and to cast *it* unto the dogs.

28 And she answered and said unto him, Yes, Lord: yet the dogs under the table eat of the children's crumbs.

29 And he said unto her, For this saying go thy way; the devil is gone out of thy daughter.

30 And when she was come to her house, she found the devil gone out, and her daughter laid upon the bed.

—MARK 7:24–30

MIRACLES OF RESURRECTION

Miracles of Resurrection

Previous page:

Christ's Resurrection is prefigured by His Transfiguration on Mount Tabor, flanked by Moses and Elijah and witnessed by the disciples Peter, James and John.

For believers in Christ, the sovereign sign of His unique nature—both human and divine—is His victory over death, as seen in the Resurrection. The gospels tell us that during his life on Earth, he raised at least three people from the dead: the twelve-year-old daughter of Jairus, the young man identified as the widow of Nain's only son, and Lazarus. These accounts have inspired people for almost two thousand years, giving rise to the hope that bodily death is not the end of human existence, but the doorway into a new kind of life characterized by freedom from sorrow, pain, and poverty. Reports of near-death experiences through the ages, from every faith and culture, support the hope that life as we know it is only a beginning.

A moving story of a child's resurrection occurs in three of the Gospels, including the account from Mark that appears here. Jairus, described as "a ruler of the synagogue," whose daughter is dying, comes to Christ and begs him to "lay thy hands on her, that she may be healed." On the way to Jairus' house, a party of mourners meets them with the news that the child has died, but Christ reassures the stricken father. When they arrive, Christ dismisses the mourners, telling them that the child is not dead, but asleep. Then he goes into the girl's room with her parents, takes her hand, and gently calls her back to life. It is significant that the girl is twelve years old, on the threshold of maturity. Bearing a child was the highest honor and blessing to a Jewish woman and her family. Barrenness was a stigma, and the failure of a family line, a tragedy. Had Jairus and his wife lost their child, her promise as a daughter of Abraham, in whose descendants "all families of the earth [shall] be blessed," would never have come to fruition.

The well-loved story of Lazarus also refers to death as sleep. After hearing of the illness of Lazarus while they were traveling, Christ tells His disciples prophetically: "This sickness is not unto death, but for the glory of God, that the

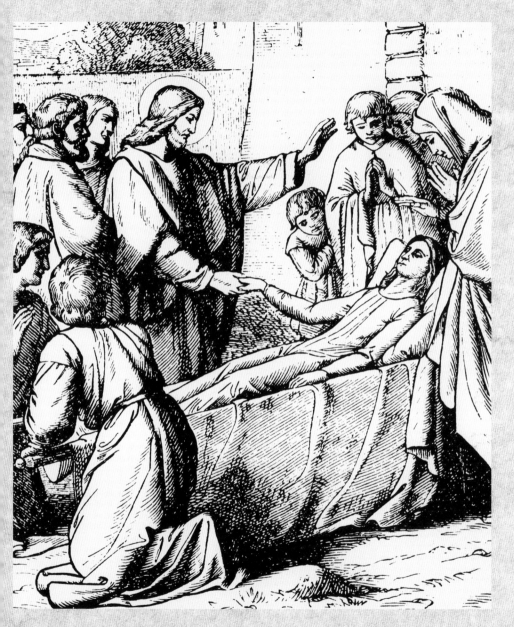

Son of God might be glorified thereby." Here, shortly before His own death, Christ prepares His disciples for the miracle of resurrection and openly declares Himself to be the Son of God. Soon afterward, they receive word that Lazarus has died and return to Bethany, outside Jerusalem. Their

Above: The grieving widow of Nain sees her son's life restored on the way to his burial.

friends Martha and Mary, the sisters of Lazarus, express their faith in Christ as the Messiah and tell him sorrowfully that their brother would not have died had He been there. He reassures them with the words that have consoled so many mourners: "I am the resurrection and the life; he that believeth in me though he were dead, yet shall he live." Then they proceed to the tomb, and Christ weeps and prays, "groaning in himself" as the power of God flows through Him. He calls loudly, "Lazarus, come forth," and His friend emerges from the tomb, still wrapped in the grave clothes of the Eastern burial rite. Christ commands the awestruck bystanders: "Loose him, and let him go."

This event prefigures Christ's own Resurrection, whereby the Creator confirmed Him as the Son of God and savior of the world. The words "Loose him, and let him go" clearly refer to the freedom from sin and death conferred by Christ's sacrificial act. Christians believe that at the hour of His death, the Holy Spirit of God was poured out upon the world, and the course of human history was irreversibly altered. Three days later, when the grieving women came to Christ's tomb to anoint His body, they were greeted by two angels who asked them: "Why seek ye the living among the dead?" During the forty days before Christ ascended "unto my Father," he made miraculous appearances to Mary Magdalen and "doubting" Thomas, among others, as proof of his Resurrection.

Christ's Resurrection was the good news that a handful of chosen followers proceeded to spread throughout the known world. It would be embraced by millions and would affect the lives of countless others who might never have heard the name of Christ. Renowned saints would carry it forward, and it would be lived out by simple people whose names are known to God alone. In the words taken down by the English mystic Julian of Norwich, who experienced a series of revelations from Christ in 1373: "I may make all things well; I can make all things well, and I will make all things well."

Opposite: The apostles (foreground) were overcome by awe when Christ was transfigured on Mount Tabor and a voice from heaven declared "This is my son." The radiance emanating from Christ prefigures His Resurrection in this vision painted by Fra Angelico c. 1441–43.

THE DAUGHTER OF JAIRUS

Below: Jesus turned the anguish of this twelve-year-old's parents into joy and astonishment by bringing her miraculously back to life.

22 And, behold, there cometh one of the rulers of the synagogue, Jairus by name; and when he saw him, he fell at his feet,

23 And besought him greatly, saying, My little daughter lieth at the point of death: *I pray thee*, come and lay thy hands on her, that she may be healed; and she shall live.

24 And *Jesus* went with him; and much people followed him, and thronged him.

*   *   *

35 While he yet spake, there came from the ruler of the synagogue's *house certain* which said, Thy daughter is dead: why troublest thou the Master any further?

36 As soon as Jesus heard the word that was spoken, he saith unto the ruler of the synagogue, Be not afraid, only believe.

37 And he suffered no man to follow him, save Peter, and James, and John the brother of James.

38 And he cometh to the house of the ruler of the synagogue, and seeth the tumult, and them that wept and wailed greatly.

39 And when he was come in, he saith unto them, Why make ye this ado and weep? the damsel is not dead but sleepeth.

40 And they laughed him to scorn. But when he had put them all out, he taketh the father and the mother of the damsel, and them that were with him, and entereth in where the damsel was lying.

41 And he took the damsel by the hand, and said unto her. Talitha cumi; which is, being interpreted, Damsel, I say unto thee, arise.

42 And straightway the damsel arose, and walked; for she was *of the age* of twelve years. And they were astonished with a great astonishment.

43 And he charged them straitly that no man should know it; and commanded that something should be given her to eat.

—MARK 5:22–24, 35–43

Above: The pre-eminent sign of Christ's divine nature was His power to restore the dead to life, as depicted in this illumination from a medieval Book of Hours.

THE RAISING OF LAZARUS

20 Then Martha, as soon as she heard that Jesus was coming, went and met him: but Mary sat *still* in the house.

21 Then said Martha unto Jesus, Lord, if thou hadst been here, my brother had not died.

22 But I know, that even now, whatsoever thou wilt ask of God, God will give *it* thee.

23 Jesus saith unto her, Thy brother shall rise again.

24 Martha saith unto him, I know that he shall rise again in the resurrection at the last day.

25 Jesus said unto her, I am the resurrection, and the life: he that believeth in me, though he were dead, yet shall he live:

26 And whosoever liveth and believeth in me shall never die. Believest thou this?

27 She saith unto him, Yea, Lord: I believe that thou art the Christ, the Son of God, which should come into the world.

28 And when she had so said, she went her way, and called Mary her sister secretly, saying, The Master is come, and calleth for thee.

29 As soon as she heard *that*, she arose quickly, and came unto him.

30 Now Jesus was not yet come into the town, but was in that place where Martha met him.

31 The Jews then which were with her in the house, and comforted her, when they saw Mary, that she rose up hastily and went out, followed her, saying, She goeth unto the grave to weep there.

32 Then when Mary was come where Jesus was, and saw him, she fell down at his feet, saying unto him, Lord, if thou hadst been here, my brother had not died.

33 When Jesus therefore saw her weeping, and the Jews also weeping which came with her, he groaned in the spirit, and was troubled,

34 And said, Where have ye laid him? They said unto him, Lord, come and see.

35 Jesus wept.

36 Then said the Jews, Behold how he loved him!

37 And some of them said, Could not this man, which opened the eyes of the blind, have caused that even this man should not have died?

38 Jesus therefore again groaning in himself cometh to the grave. It was a cave, and a stone lay upon it.

39 Jesus said, Take ye away the stone. Martha, the sister of him that was dead, saith unto him, Lord, by this time he stinketh: for he hath been *dead* four days.

40 Jesus saith unto her, Said I not unto thee, that, if thou wouldest believe, thou shouldest see the glory of God?

Above: Lazarus rises from his tomb swathed in graveclothes in this haunting evocation of the scene.

41 Then they took away the stone *from the place* where the dead was laid. And Jesus lifted up *his* eyes, and said, Father, I thank thee that thou hast heard me.

42 And I knew that thou hearest me always: but because of the people which stand by I said *it*, that they may believe that thou hast sent me.

43 And when he thus had spoken, he cried with a loud voice, Lazarus, come forth.

44 And he that was dead came forth, bound hand and foot with graveclothes: and his face was bound about with a napkin. Jesus saith unto them, Loose him, and let him go.

—JOHN 11:20–44

Above: A stark portrait by Caravaggio of Mary and Martha grieving over their brother Lazarus as Christ speaks the word of command that will raise him from the dead.

THE RESURRECTION OF CHRIST

1 Now upon the first day of the week, very early in the morning, they came unto the sepulchre, bringing the spices which they had prepared, and certain *others* with them.

2 And they found the stone rolled away from the sepulchre.

3 And they entered in, and found not the body of the Lord Jesus.

4 And it came to pass, as they were much perplexed thereabout, behold, two men stood by them in shining garments:

5 And as they were afraid, and bowed down *their* faces to the earth, they said unto them, Why seek ye the living among the dead?

6 He is not here, but is risen: remember how he spake unto you when he was yet in Galilee,

7 Saying, The Son of man must be delivered into the hands of sinful men, and be crucified, and the third day rise again.

8   And they remembered his words,

9   And returned from the sepulchre, and told all these things unto the eleven, and to all the rest.

10 It was Mary Magdalene, and Joanna, and Mary *the mother* of James, and other *women that were* with them, which told these things unto the apostles.

11 And their words seemed to them as idle tales, and they believed them not.

12 Then arose Peter, and ran unto the sepulchre; and stooping down, he beheld the linen clothes laid by themselves, and departed, wondering in himself at that which was come to pass.

—LUKE 24:1–12

Left: *The Risen Christ, portrayed by Fra Bartolommeo with the staff of authority upholding the orb of the world crowned by the cross. He is flanked by the four Evangelists. The chalice supporting the pedestal symbolizes Christ's blood poured out for salvation (from the Hebrew word for "homecoming").*

NOLI ME TANGERE: "TOUCH ME NOT"

11 But Mary stood without at the sepulchre weeping: and as she wept, she stooped down, *and looked* into the sepulchre,

12 And seeth two angels in white sitting, the one at the head, and the other at the feet, where the body of Jesus had lain.

13 And they say unto her, Woman, why weepest thou? She saith unto them, Because they have taken away my Lord, and I know not where they have laid him.

14 And when she had thus said, she turned herself back, and saw Jesus standing, and knew not that it was Jesus.

15 Jesus saith unto her, Woman, why weepest thou? whom seekest thou? She, supposing him to be the gardener,

Below: Mary Magdalene's joy upon recognizing Jesus brought back to life is captured in this moving portrayal by Fra Angelico.

saith unto him, Sir, if thou have borne him hence, tell me where thou hast laid him, and I will take him away.

16 Jesus saith unto her, Mary. She turned herself, and saith unto him, Rabboni; which is to say, Master.

17 Jesus saith unto her, Touch me not; for I am not yet ascended to my Father: but go to my brethren, and say unto them, I ascend unto my Father, and your Father; and *to* my God, and your God.

18 Mary Magdalene came and told the disciples that she had seen the Lord, and *that* he had spoken these things unto her.

—JOHN 20:11–18

DOUBTING THOMAS

24 But Thomas, one of the twelve, called Didymus, was not with them when Jesus came.

25 The other disciples therefore said unto him, We have seen the Lord. But he said unto them, Except I shall see in his hands the print of the nails, and put my finger into the print of the nails, and thrust my hand into his side, I will not believe.

26 And after eight days again his disciples were within, and Thomas with them: *then* came Jesus, the doors being shut, and stood in the midst, and said, Peace *be* unto you.

27 Then saith he to Thomas, Reach hither thy finger, and behold my hands; and reach hither thy hand, and thrust *it* into my side: and be not faithless, but believing.

28 And Thomas answered and said unto him, My Lord and my God.

29 Jesus saith unto him, Thomas, because thou hast seen me, thou hast believed: blessed *are* they that have not seen, and *yet* have believed.

—JOHN 20:24–29

INDEX OF MIRACLES

Page numbers in *italics* refer to illustrations.

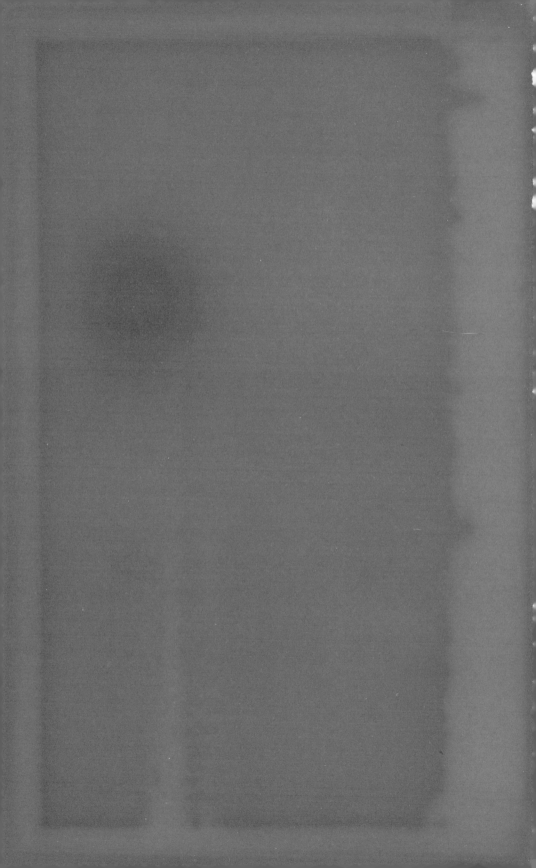

The Passion of the CHRIST

The Passion of the
CHRIST

CLARE HAWORTH-MADEN
Editor

Saraband

Page 1: *Christ on the cross, by Fra Angelico.*

Page 2: *Giotto's depiction of the fateful kiss of Judas.*

Page 3: *A detail from a Fra Angelico panel showing Christ being lifted from the cross.*

Published by Saraband (Scotland) Limited,
The Arthouse, 752–756 Argyle Street,
Glasgow G3 8UJ, Scotland
hermes@saraband.net

Copyright © 2004 Saraband (Scotland) Ltd.

ISBN: 1-887354-38-7

Printed in China

10 9 8 7 6 5 4 3 2

Acknowledgements

Extracts from the Authorized Version of the Bible (The King James Bible), the rights in which are vested in the Crown, are reproduced by permission of the Crown's Patentee, Cambridge University Press.

The publisher would like to thank the following people for their assistance in the preparation of this book: Deborah Hayes, Phoebe Wong. Grateful acknowledgment is also made for the illustrations featured in this book, which are reproduced courtesy of Planet Art, with the exception of the following:

© **2002 Arttoday.com, Inc:** 16, 18, 31, 32, 46, 47, 48, 49; **Saraband Image Library:** 14, 15, 21, 28, 29, 34, 38, 40, 41, 42, 44, 45, 50, 54, 57, 69, 71, 78.

Bibliography

Douglas, J. D. & Tenney, Merrill C., *NIV Compact Dictionary of the Bible*, Hodder & Stoughton, London, 1989.

Farmer, David, *Oxford Dictionary of Saints*, Oxford University Press, Oxford, 1996.

Fisher, Sally, *The Square Halo and Other Mysteries of Western Art*, Harry N. Abrams, Inc., New York, 1995.

Pawson, David, *Unlocking the Bible Omnibus*, Collins, London, 2003.

The Holy Bible, the King James Version.

The Lion Handbook to the Bible, Lion Publishing plc, Oxford, 1983.

Contents

Introduction

F or even hereunto were ye called: because Christ also suffered for us, leaving us an example, that ye should follow in his steps.

—PETER 2:21

The resignation with which Christ endured the most horrific of deaths in order to redeem humankind has awed Christians for over two millennia. And while martyrs have literally followed in His steps, Christ's example has inspired many ordinary people to find the courage to bear their sufferings in this world in the hope of being rewarded with everlasting life in the next.

The Passion as Recounted in the Gospels

The terrible details of Christ's Passion (a word derived from the Church Latin *passio*, "suffering") following His triumphant entry into Jerusalem are described in each of the four gospels of the New Testament. Although they tell essentially the same tale, Matthew, Mark, Luke, and John's accounts vary slightly, maybe partly because they were writing for different audiences.

Matthew is believed to have been Matthew Levi, the tax-collector and one of Christ's twelve apostles, and it is likely that his gospel was aimed at Jews who had become Christians, just as he had. This is why he identifies Christ as the king of the Jews and long-awaited Messiah, as prophesied in the Old Testament.

Scholars have associated Mark with John Mark, a companion of Barnabas, Paul, and, most significantly, Peter, the first pope, on whose recollections the gospel is traditionally said to be based. The evangelical, action-packed tone of Mark's gospel, and emphasis on Christ being the "son of man," suggests that it was targeted at Roman Gentiles whom he hoped to convert to Christianity. It is thought that Mark's gospel is the oldest, and that it was later expanded upon by Matthew and Luke.

Another associate of Paul was the physician Luke, a Syrian from Antioch, and probably the author of Luke's gospel. Luke states that his gospel is drawn from the reminiscences of "eyewitnesses, and ministers of the word" for Theophilus, "That thou mightest know the certainty of those things, wherein thou hast been instructed" (Luke 1:2–4). As well as being a historical testimony composed for an interested and educated Greek, Luke's gospel is evangelical in its portrayal of Christ as the "savior" of humankind.

"The disciple whom Jesus loved," "This is the disciple which testifieth of these things, and wrote these things," it is stated in John 21:20 and 21:24. The author of John's gospel is consequently one of the apostles who was closest to Christ, and in all likelihood the fisherman son of Zebedee. Although it is a first-hand account, John's gospel is more of commentary and interpretation than the previous three (whose similarity has caused them to be termed the "synoptic gospels"), and was almost certainly the last to be set down. It is clear that John's purpose in writing his gospel was to strengthen the faith of existing believers in the "son of God."

THE EVENTS OF CHRIST'S PASSION

The haunting story of Christ's Passion starts with Christ entering Jerusalem on a donkey, the sound of "Hosannas" ringing in His ears, yet in the knowledge that it is only a matter of days before He will be betrayed and crucified.

It continues with the Last Supper, which Matthew, Mark, and Luke—but not John—say was the Passover meal with which Jews commemorate the Exodus and their deliverance from the Babylonian slavery. Unleavened bread and

wine are ritually consumed, and it is on this occasion that Christ institutes the Holy Eucharist by telling His disciples that the bread is His body, and the wine, His blood, which will soon be broken and spilled. (Poignantly, just as Jews sacrifice a lamb for the Passover meal in memory of the lamb's blood that their forebears daubed on their doorposts to save their firstborns from God's vengeance on the Egyptians, so Christ is the "Lamb of God" who will be sacrificed for humanity's salvation.) At this meal, John tells us that Christ washes His disciples' feet as a demonstration of humility, but also identifies Judas as His betrayer and predicts Peter's triple denial.

With the conclusion of the Last Supper, Christ leads His disciples to the Garden of Gethsemane and asks Peter, James, and John to keep watch while He prays to God to protect and sanctify His followers. They fall asleep, but nothing can in any case prevent the arrival of Judas with a band of men charged with arresting Christ by the Jewish priests, officials, and elders, and his traitorous identification of Christ with a kiss.

Above: Tintoretto's dramatic depiction of the Last Supper vividly evokes the occasion when Jesus first introduced His disciples to the sacrament of the Eucharist (which some Protestants call the "Lord's Supper").

Opposite: Christ's agony on the cross was a fate reserved only for those who were deemed to deserve the cruelest form of punishment.

Christ is seized and taken before Caiaphas, the high priest in charge of the Sanhedrin (the supreme Jewish council or court), whose politically motivated members are hostile to the accused. In the meantime, Peter, in fear of arrest himself, indeed denies Christ three times. Christ is pronounced guilty of blasphemy, which, under Jewish law, merits the death penalty, but with Judea under Roman rule, the Sanhedrin is not empowered to execute its verdict, which is why Christ is taken before Pontius Pilate, the Roman procurator, or governor. Luke alone testifies that Pilate sends Christ on to Herod Antipas (the governor of Christ's home province of Galilee who is visiting Jerusalem for the Passover festival), who returns Him to Pilate. All agree, however, that it is with Pilate that Christ's fate is sealed when He admits to being the "king of the Jews," which, as the Jews point out, is a treasonous assertion that an appointee of the Roman emperor cannot overlook ("If thou let this man go, thou art not Caesar's friend: whosoever maketh himself a king speaketh against Caesar." John 19:12.) Nevertheless reluctant to condemn Christ to death, Pilate offers to release either Him or the criminal Barabbas, in accordance with his Passover practice of pardoning a prisoner. But the Jews present call for Barabbas to be freed, and for Christ to be crucified, and Pilate has no option but to concede.

Christ's physical suffering now begins. He is stripped, beaten, crowned with thorns, garbed in a robe the color of royalty, and forced to hold a reed scepter as He is cruelly mocked. Then He is sent for crucifixion (only John asserts that He Himself carries the cross on which He will die, the other three gospels assigning that role to Simon the Cyrenian) at Golgotha, or Calvary. Crucifixion is an appalling form of torture and execution that the Romans reserved for the most despicable of criminals, and Christ's hands and feet are duly nailed to the cross and a sign is erected above His head that reads *Iesus Nazarenus Rex Iudaeorum*, the Latin for "Jesus of Nazareth, King of the Jews." After six hours, death mercifully releases Christ from His agony.

The story of Christ's mortal life ends with Joseph of Arimathea, a prominent Jew and covert Christian, begging Pilate for permission to remove Christ's body from the cross. Pilate agrees, and the corpse is wrapped in a linen shroud and laid in a nearby sepulcher. Yet three days later, the sepulcher is found empty, and the resurrected Christ reveals Himself to various of His initially incredulous disciples. His work on Earth done, Christ finally ascends to heaven to be at the side of His divine father.

The Agony and the Ecstasy

Although the gospels' harrowing accounts of Christ's Passion have the power to shock, move, and humble the most detached of readers, their impact on those who have dedicated themselves to Christ can be truly extraordinary. It is recorded, for example, that St. Francis of Assisi (1181–1226) developed stigmata—five wounds that correspond to those inflicted on Christ during His Passion—in 1224, the first documented instance of the phenomenon.

Another pious stigmatic was the German Augustinian nun Sister Anna Katharina Emmerich (1774–1824), an ecstatic who recounted her revelations from God to the German writer Clemens Brentano (1778–1842). These were first published in 1833 as *Das bittere Leiden unseres Herrn Jesu Christi. Nach dem Betrachtungen der gottseligen Anna Katharina Emmerich* (*The Dolorous Passion of Our Lord Jesus Christ According to the Meditations of the Blessed Anne Catherine Emmerich*), and continue to inspire the faithful.

There is also a religious order devoted to the Passion, the Congregation of the Barefooted Clerics of the Most Holy Cross and Passion of Our Lord Jesus Christ, which was founded in 1720 in Italy by St. Paul of the Cross (1694–1775) in response to a vision. In addition to making vows of poverty, charity, and obedience, Passionists swear that they will promote a devotion to Christ's Passion in others.

How Ordinary Christians Commemorate the Passion

Christ's Passion is at the forefront of every practicing Christian's mind during Holy Week, which begins on Palm Sunday and culminates on Easter Sunday. On Palm Sunday, palm crosses are distributed among congregations in remembrance of Christ's entry into Jerusalem, when, according to John 12:12–13, the people hailed Christ with palm branches. Maundy Thursday is the day on which the disadvantaged are traditionally invited into churches to have their feet washed by priests in emulation of Christ's demonstration of humility at the Last Supper. And on Good Friday, the Christian Church mourns the crucifixion of Christ, His resurrection being celebrated two days later, on Easter Sunday.

A popular tradition of performing passion plays, in which members of the lay Christian community re-enact the tragic events of the Passion, developed during the Middle Ages in Europe. But because many gradually lost their pious purpose and developed into scurrilous, anticlerical farces, they were increasingly banned from the sixteenth century onward. One that has survived, however, has been performed by the Bavarian villagers of Oberammergau, in Germany, every ten years since 1634, in accordance with a vow made to God in the hope that they would thereby be spared the Black Death.

Above: Botticelli's Lamentation over the Dead Christ *(c. 1490) is a tempera panel in the Alte Pinakothek in Munich, Germany.*

THE WAY OF THE CROSS

The fervent devotion that the Passion aroused in medieval Christians remains alive today, often being reinforced by the Roman Catholic medium of the Way of the Cross, also known as the Stations of the Cross, *Via Dolorosa*, or *Via Crucis*, a series of fourteen tableaux that portray aspects of Christ's agony, as follows.

> Christ is condemned to death.
> Christ carries his cross.
> Christ falls for the first time.
> Christ meets his mother.
> Simon the Cyrenian carries the cross.
> Veronica wipes Christ's face.
> Christ falls for the second time.
> Christ meets the women of Jerusalem.
> Christ falls for the third time.
> Christ is stripped.
> Christ is nailed to the cross.
> Christ dies on the cross.
> Christ is taken down from the cross.
> Christ is laid in the sepulcher.

Opposite and right:
While John reported that Jesus carried His own cross to the place designated for His crucifixion, the other three gospels relate that Simon the Cyrenian (opposite) bore the cross for Him.

The origin of the Way of the Cross can be traced back to St. Francis of Assisi, who traveled to Egypt in 1219 on a mission to convert the Saracen sultan to Christianity. Although the sultan refused to abandon Islam, he did grant the Franciscan order guardianship of the Holy Sepulcher in Jerusalem, the city having been under the sultanate's control since 1187. In 1342, the Franciscans' guardianship was extended to the Holy Places in Jerusalem, the ultimate place of pilgrimage for Christians, which few had any hope of visiting. In 1686, Pope Innocent XI permitted the Franciscans to mount representations of the Stations of the Cross in their churches, and decreed that meditating on each would merit an indulgence, a privilege that Pope Benedict XIII broadened to embrace all faithful Roman Catholics in 1726. Now represented in most Roman Catholic churches, the Way of the Cross therefore offers a spiritual pilgrimage to those who are unable to visit the Holy Places in person.

The Stations, whose number was standardized by Pope Clement XII in 1731, include certain events that are absent from the gospels, such as Veronica's wiping of Christ's face, causing His blood-stained image to be miraculously imprinted upon her cloth. Veronica was first mentioned in the fourth- to fifth-century "Gospel of Nicodemus," and a relic that is said to be her "veil" has indeed been preserved in St. Peter's in Rome since the eighth century. Historians nevertheless speculate that because *vera icona* is the Latin for "true image," Veronica's existence was invented to underline the relic's authenticity.

THE PAGES THAT FOLLOW

Over the following pages, selected extracts from all four gospels (drawn from the King James Version of the New Testament) narrate the inexorable course of Christ's Passion. But because each gospel differs in content and style, readers are urged to read Matthew, Mark, Luke, and John for themselves in order to gain the fullest possible picture of Christ's suffering.

"I Am Come a Light into the World"

CHRIST'S ENTRY INTO JERUSALEM

Previous page and below: Zechariah, the prophet to whom Matthew refers in verse 21:4, prophesied that the Messiah would enter Jerusalem riding on an ass (Zechariah 9:9), as portrayed below by Fra Angelico.

1   And when they drew nigh unto Jerusalem, and were come to Bethphage, unto the mount of Olives, then sent Jesus two disciples,

2   Saying unto them, Go into the village over against you, and straightway ye shall find an ass tied, and a colt with her: loose *them*, and bring *them* unto me.

3   And if any *man* say ought unto you, ye shall say, The Lord hath need of them; and straightway he will send them.

4   All this was done, that it might be fulfilled which was spoken by the prophet, saying,

5   Tell ye the daughter of Sion, Behold, thy King cometh unto thee, meek, and sitting upon an ass, and a colt the foal of an ass.

6   And the disciples went, and did as Jesus commanded them,

7   And brought the ass, and the colt, and put on them their clothes, and they set *him* thereon.

8   And a very great multitude spread their garments in the way; others cut down branches from the trees, and strawed *them* in the way.

9   And the multitudes that went before, and that followed, cried, saying, Hosanna to the Son of David: Blessed *is* he that cometh in the name of the Lord; Hosanna in the highest.

10 And when he was come into Jerusalem, all the city was moved, saying, Who is this?

11 And the multitude said, This is Jesus the prophet of Nazareth of Galilee.

12 And Jesus went into the temple of God, and cast out all them that sold and bought in the temple, and overthrew the tables of the moneychangers, and the seats of them that sold doves,

13 And said unto them, It is written, My house shall be called the house of prayer; but ye have made it a den of thieves.

14 And the blind and the lame came to him in the temple; and he healed them.

15 And when the chief priests and scribes saw the wonderful things that he did, and the children crying in the temple, and saying, Hosanna to the son of David; they were sore displeased,

16 And said unto him, Hearest thou what these say? And Jesus saith unto them, Yea; have ye never read, Out of the mouth of babes and sucklings thou hast perfected praise?

17 And he left them, and went out of the city into Bethany; and he lodged there.

—MATTHEW 21:1–17

CHRIST PREDICTS HIS CRUCIFIXION

1 And it came to pass, when Jesus had finished all these sayings, he said unto his disciples,
2 Ye know that after two days is *the feast* of the passover, and the Son of man is betrayed to be crucified.

—MATTHEW 26:1–2

"I CAME NOT TO JUDGE THE WORLD, BUT TO SAVE THE WORLD"

23 And Jesus answered them, saying, The hour is come, that the Son of man should be glorified.
24 Verily, verily, I say unto you, Except a corn of wheat fall into the ground and die, it abideth alone: but if it die, it bringeth forth much fruit.
25 He that loveth his life shall lose it; and he that hateth his life in this world shall keep it unto life eternal.
26 If any man serve me, let him follow me; and where I am, there shall also my servant be: if any man serve me, him will *my* Father honour.
27 Now is my soul troubled; and what shall I say? Father, save me from this hour: but for this cause came I unto this hour.
28 Father, glorify thy name. Then came there a voice from heaven, *saying*, I have both glorified *it*, and will glorify *it* again.
29 The people therefore, that stood by, and heard *it*, said that it thundered: others said, An angel spake to him.
30 Jesus answered and said, This voice came not because of me, but for your sakes.
31 Now is the judgment of this world: now shall the prince of this world be cast out.

32 And I, if I be lifted up from the earth, will draw all *men* unto me.

33 This he said, signifying what death he should die.

34 The people answered him, We have heard out of the law that Christ abideth for ever: and how sayest thou, The Son of man must be lifted up? who is this Son of man?

35 Then Jesus said unto them, Yet a little while is the light with you. Walk while ye have the light, lest darkness come upon you: for he that walketh in darkness knoweth not whither he goeth.

36 While ye have light, believe in the light, that ye may be the children of light. These things spake Jesus, and departed, and did hide himself from them.

Below: *John (12:13) relates that the people of Jerusalem "took branches of palm trees" before going forth to meet Jesus. In Jewish belief, the* lulav *("palm branch" in Hebrew) can symbolize God, as well as a righteous man (*tzaddik*).*

37 But though he had done so many miracles before them, yet they believed not on him:

38 That the saying of Esaias the prophet might be fulfilled, which he spake, Lord, who hath believed our report? and to whom hath the arm of the Lord been revealed?

39 Therefore they could not believe, because that Esaias said again,

40 He hath blinded their eyes, and hardened their heart; that they should not see with *their* eyes, nor understand with *their* heart, and be converted, and I should heal them.

41 These things said Esaias, when he saw his glory, and spake of him.

42 Nevertheless among the chief rulers also many believed on him; but because of the Pharisees they did not confess *him*, lest they should be put out of the synagogue:

43 For they loved the praise of men more than the praise of God.

44 Jesus cried and said, He that believeth on me, believeth not on me, but on him that sent me.

45 And he that seeth me seeth him that sent me.

46 I am come a light into the world, that whosoever believeth on me should not abide in darkness.

47 And if any man hear my words, and believe not, I judge him not: for I came not to judge the world, but to save the world.

48 He that rejecteth me, and receiveth not my words, hath one that judgeth him: the word that I have spoken, the same shall judge him in the last day.

49 For I have not spoken of myself; but the Father which sent me, he gave me a commandment, what I should say, and what I should speak.

50 And I know that his commandment is life everlasting: whatsoever I speak therefore, even as the Father said unto me, so I speak.

—JOHN 12:23–50

"Behold, the Hour Cometh"

THE LAST SUPPER

Previous page and below: The Last Supper has been illustrated by many notable artists, including Titian (previous page) and Leonardo da Vinci (below), whose famous fresco captures the moment when Jesus shocks His disciples by stating that one of them will betray Him.

12 And the first day of unleavened bread, when they killed the passover, his disciples said unto him, Where wilt thou that we go and prepare that thou mayest eat the passover?

13 And he sendeth forth two of his disciples, and saith unto them, Go ye into the city, and there shall meet you a man bearing a pitcher of water: follow him.

14 And wheresoever he shall go in, say ye to the goodman of the house, The Master saith, Where is the guestchamber, where I shall eat the passover with my disciples?

15 And he will shew you a large upper room furnished *and* prepared: there make ready for us.

16 And his disciples went forth, and came into the city, and found as he had said unto them: and they made ready the passover.

17 And in the evening he cometh with the twelve.

—MARK 14:12–17

"Take, Eat; This Is My Body"

20 Now when the even was come, he sat down with the twelve.

21 And as they did eat, he said, Verily I say unto you, that one of you shall betray me.

22 And they were exceeding sorrowful, and began every one of them to say unto him, Lord, is it I?

23 And he answered and said, He that dippeth *his* hand with me in the dish, the same shall betray me.

24 The Son of man goeth as it is written of him: but woe unto that man by whom the Son of man is betrayed! it had been good for that man if he had not been born.

25 Then Judas, which betrayed him, answered and said, Master, is it I? He said unto him, Thou hast said.

26 And as they were eating, Jesus took bread, and blessed *it*, and brake *it*, and gave *it* to the disciples, and said, Take, eat; this is my body.

Right: *Giotto's exquisite depiction of the Last Supper, a fresco painted c. 1304–06, shows a serene Jesus with the disciples who are "exceeding sorrowful."*

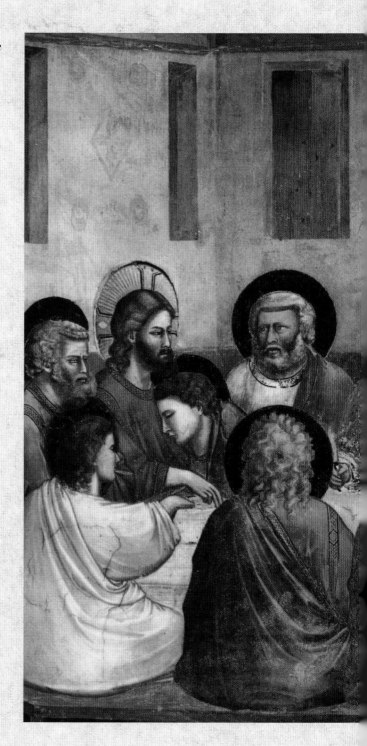

27 And he took the cup, and gave thanks, and gave *it* to them, saying, Drink ye all of it;

28 For this is my blood of the new testament, which is shed for many for the remission of sins.

29 But I say unto you, I will not drink henceforth of this fruit of the vine, until that day when I drink it new with you in my Father's kingdom.

—MATTHEW 26:20–29

Below: *During the Last Supper, Jesus anticipated His death by comparing the bread and wine that He urged the disciples to consume with His body and blood, which would soon be broken and shed for the remission of humankind's sins.*

CHRIST WASHES THE DISCIPLES' FEET

2 And supper being ended, the devil having now put into the heart of Judas Iscariot, Simon's *son*, to betray him;

3 Jesus knowing that the Father had given all things into his hands, and that he was come from God, and went to God;

4 He riseth from supper, and laid aside his garments; and took a towel, and girded himself.

5 After that he poureth water into a bason, and began to wash the disciples' feet, and to wipe *them* with the towel wherewith he was girded.

6 Then cometh he to Simon Peter: and Peter saith unto him, Lord, dost thou wash my feet?

7 Jesus answered and said unto him, What I do thou knowest not now; but thou shalt know hereafter.

8 Peter saith unto him, Thou shalt never wash my feet.

Jesus answered him, If I wash thee not, thou hast no part with me.

9 Simon Peter saith unto him, Lord, not my feet only, but also *my* hands and *my* head.

10 Jesus saith to him, He that is washed needeth not save to wash *his* feet, but is clean every whit: and ye are clean, but not all.

11 For he knew who should betray him; therefore said he, Ye are not all clean.

12 So after he had washed their feet, and had taken his garments, and was set down again, he said unto them, Know ye what I have done to you?

13 Ye call me Master and Lord: and ye say well; for *so* I am.

14 If I then, *your* Lord and Master, have washed your feet; ye also ought to wash one another's feet.

15 For I have given you an example, that ye should do as I have done to you.

16 Verily, verily, I say unto you, The servant is not greater than his lord; neither he that is sent greater than he that sent him.

17 If ye know these things, happy are ye if ye do them.

18 I speak not of you all: I know whom I have chosen: but that the scripture may be fulfilled, He that eateth bread with me hath lifted up his heel against me.

19 Now I tell you before it come, that, when it is come to pass, ye may believe that I am *he*.

20 Verily, verily, I say unto you, He that receiveth whomsoever I send receiveth me; and he that receiveth me receiveth him that sent me.

Above: *Luke (22:24) says that an argument broke out among the disciples during the Last Supper about "which of them should be accounted the greatest." John explains that by washing their feet, Jesus was teaching them about equality and humility.*

—JOHN 13:2–20

CHRIST IDENTIFIES JUDAS AS HIS BETRAYER, AND PETER AS HIS DENIER

21 When Jesus had thus said, he was troubled in spirit, and testified, and said, Verily, verily, I say unto you, that one of you shall betray me.

22 Then the disciples looked one on another, doubting of whom he spake.

23 Now there was leaning on Jesus' bosom one of his disciples, whom Jesus loved.

24 Simon Peter therefore beckoned to him, that he should ask who it should be of whom he spake.

25 He then lying on Jesus' breast saith unto him, Lord, who is it?

26 Jesus answered, He it is, to whom I shall give a sop, when I have dipped *it*. And when he had dipped the sop, he gave *it* to Judas Iscariot, *the son* of Simon.

27 And after the sop Satan entered into him. Then said Jesus unto him, That thou doest, do quickly.

28 Now no man at the table knew for what intent he spake this unto him.

29 For some *of them* thought, because Judas had the bag, that Jesus had said unto him, Buy *those things* that we have need of against the feast; or, that he should give something to the poor.

30 He then having received the sop went immediately out: and it was night.

31 Therefore, when he was gone out, Jesus said, Now is the Son of man glorified, and God is glorified in him.

32 If God be glorified in him, God shall also glorify him in himself, and shall straightway glorify him.

33 Little children, yet a little while I am with you. Ye shall seek me: and as I said unto the Jews, Whither I go, ye cannot come; so now I say to you.

34 A new commandment I give unto you, That ye love one

another; as I have loved you, that ye also love one another.

35 By this shall all *men* know that ye are my disciples, if ye have love one to another.

36 Simon Peter said unto him, Lord, whither goest thou? Jesus answered him, Whither I go, thou canst not follow me now; but thou shalt follow me afterwards.

37 Peter said unto him, Lord, why cannot I follow thee now? I will lay down my life for thy sake.

38 Jesus answered him, Wilt thou lay down thy life for my sake? Verily, verily, I say unto thee, The cock shall not crow, till thou hast denied me thrice.

—JOHN 13:21–38

CHRIST PRAYS TO GOD, THE FATHER

32 Behold, the hour cometh, yea, is now come, that ye shall be scattered, every man to his own, and shall leave me alone: and yet I am not alone, because the Father is with me.

33 These things I have spoken unto you, that in me ye might have peace. In the world ye shall have tribulation: but be of good cheer; I have overcome the world.

* * *

Below: Knowing that His days on Earth were numbered, Jesus entreated God to protect His disciples, as well as "them also which shall believe on me through their word" (John 17:20).

1 These words spake Jesus, and lifted up his eyes to heaven, and said, Father, the hour is come; glorify thy Son, that thy Son also may glorify thee:

2 As thou hast given him power over all flesh, that he should give eternal life to as many as thou hast given him.

3 And this is life eternal, that they might know thee the only true God, and Jesus Christ, whom thou hast sent.

4 I have glorified thee on the earth: I have finished the work which thou gavest me to do.

5 And now, O Father, glorify thou me with thine own self with the glory which I had with thee before the world was.

6 I have manifested thy name unto the men which thou gavest me out of the world: thine they were, and thou gavest them me; and they have kept thy word.

7 Now they have known that all things whatsoever thou hast given me are of thee.

8 For I have given unto them the words which thou gavest me; and they have received *them*,

Above: *John recounts that before making his way to the Garden of Gethsemane, Jesus raised His eyes to heaven and prayed to God, saying "I have finished the work which thou gavest me to do" (17:4).*

and have known surely that I came out from thee, and they have believed that thou didst send me.

9 I pray for them: I pray not for the world, but for them which thou hast given me; for they are thine.

10 And all mine are thine, and thine are mine; and I am glorified in them.

11 And now I am no more in the world, but these are in the world, and I come to thee. Holy Father, keep through thine own name those whom thou hast given me, that they may be one, as we *are*.

12 While I was with them in the world, I kept them in thy name: those that thou gavest me I have kept, and none

of them is lost, but the son of perdition; that the scripture might be fulfilled.

13 And now come I to thee; and these things I speak in the world, that they might have my joy fulfilled in themselves.

14 I have given them thy word; and the world hath hated them, because they are not of the world, even as I am not of the world.

15 I pray not that thou shouldest take them out of the world, but that thou shouldest keep them from the evil.

16 They are not of the world, even as I am not of the world.

17 Sanctify them through thy truth: thy word is truth.

18 As thou hast sent me into the world, even so have I also sent them into the world.

19 And for their sakes I sanctify myself, that they also might be sanctified through the truth.

20 Neither pray I for these alone, but for them also which shall believe on me through their word;

21 That they all may be one; as thou, Father, *art* in me, and I in thee, that they also may be one in us: that the world may believe that thou hast sent me.

22 And the glory which thou gavest me I have given them; that they may be one, even as we are one:

23 I in them, and thou in me, that they may be made perfect in one; and that the world may know that thou hast sent me, and hast loved them, as thou hast loved me.

24 Father, I will that they also, whom thou hast given me, be with me where I am; that they may behold my glory, which thou hast given me: for thou lovedst me before the foundation of the world.

25 O righteous Father, the world hath not known thee: but I have known thee, and these have known that thou hast sent me.

26 And I have declared unto them thy name, and will declare *it*: that the love wherewith thou hast loved me may be in them, and I in them.

—JOHN 16:32–33, 17:1–26

The Agony in the Garden of Gethsemane

"THE SON OF MAN IS BETRAYED INTO THE HANDS OF SINNERS"

36 Then cometh Jesus with them unto a place called Gethsemane, and saith unto the disciples, Sit ye here, while I go and pray yonder.

37 And he took with him Peter and the two sons of Zebedee, and began to be sorrowful and very heavy.

38 Then saith he unto them, My soul is exceeding sorrowful, even unto death: tarry ye here, and watch with me.

39 And he went a little further, and fell on his face, and prayed, saying, O my Father, if it be possible, let this cup pass from me: nevertheless not as I will, but as thou *wilt*.

Opposite and below: Peter, James, and John fell asleep in the Garden of Gethsemane as the agonized Jesus prayed to God, who sent an angel (opposite). Below, Mantegna's The Agony in the Garden.

40 And he cometh unto the disciples, and findeth them asleep, and saith unto Peter, What, could ye not watch with me one hour?

41 Watch and pray, that ye enter not into temptation: the spirit indeed *is* willing, but the flesh *is* weak.

42 He went away again the second time, and prayed, saying, O my Father, if this cup may not pass away from me, except I drink it, thy will be done.

43 And he came and found them asleep again: for their eyes were heavy.

44 And he left them, and went away again, and prayed the third time, saying the same words.

45 Then cometh he to his disciples, and saith unto them, Sleep on now, and take *your* rest: behold, the hour is at hand, and the Son of man is betrayed into the hands of sinners.

46 Rise, let us be going: behold, he is at hand that doth betray me.

—MATTHEW 26:36–46

Above: *According to Luke 22:44, Jesus suffered such psychological agony while praying to God in the Garden of Gethsemane that "his sweat was as it were great drops of blood falling down to the ground."*

THE KISS
OF JUDAS

JESUS IS BETRAYED

Previous page and below: *Judas had told his armed escort that he would identify Jesus by greeting Him with a kiss. Jesus was in no doubt of the significance of the gesture: "Judas, betrayest thou the Son of man with a kiss?" (Luke 22:48).*

43 And immediately, while he yet spake, cometh Judas, one of the twelve, and with him a great multitude with swords and staves, from the chief priests and the scribes and the elders.

44 And he that betrayed him had given them a token, saying, Whomsoever I shall kiss, that same is he; take him, and lead *him* away safely.

45 And as soon as he was come, he goeth straightway to him, and saith, Master, master; and kissed him.

—MARK 14:43–45

CHRIST'S ARREST

"THEN CAME THEY, AND LAID HANDS ON JESUS"

Previous page:
Giotto's depiction of the betrayal that led to Christ's arrest.

Below: *The servant's ear is severed (Matthew 26:51).*

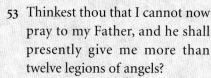

50 And Jesus said unto him, Friend, wherefore art thou come? Then came they, and laid hands on Jesus and took him.

51 And, behold, one of them which were with Jesus stretched out his hand, and drew his sword, and struck a servant of the high priest's, and smote off his ear.

52 Then said Jesus unto him, Put up again thy sword into his place: for all they that take the sword shall perish with the sword.

53 Thinkest thou that I cannot now pray to my Father, and he shall presently give me more than twelve legions of angels?

54 But how then shall the scriptures be fulfilled, that thus it must be?

55 In that same hour said Jesus to the multitudes, Are ye come out as against a thief with swords and staves for to take me? I sat daily with you teaching in the temple, and ye laid no hold on me.

56 But all this was done, that the scriptures of the prophets might be fulfilled. Then all the disciples forsook him, and fled.

—MATTHEW 26:50–56

CHRIST IS CONDEMNED AND DENIED

CHRIST IS BROUGHT BEFORE THE HIGH PRIEST CAIAPHAS

Previous page: The bound Jesus is depicted standing before Annas and his son-in-law, the high priest Caiaphas.

Below: While Jesus was in the presence of the high priest, Peter denied Him three times.

53 And they led Jesus away to the high priest: and with him were assembled all the chief priests and the elders and the scribes.

54 And Peter followed him afar off, even into the palace of the high priest: and he sat with the servants, and warmed himself at the fire.

55 And the chief priests and all the council sought for witness against Jesus to put him to death; and found none.

56 For many bare false witness against him, but their witness agreed not together.

57 And there arose certain, and bare false witness against him, saying,

58 We heard him say, I will destroy this temple that is made with hands, and within three days I will build another made without hands.

59 But neither so did their witness agree together.

60 And the high priest stood up in the midst, and asked Jesus, saying, Answerest thou nothing? what *is it which* these witness against thee?

61 But he held his peace, and answered nothing. Again the high priest asked him, and said unto him, Art thou the Christ, the Son of the Blessed?

62 And Jesus said, I am: and ye shall see the Son of man sitting on the right hand of power, and coming in the clouds of heaven.

63 Then the high priest rent his clothes, and saith, What need we any further witnesses?

64 Ye have heard the blasphemy: what think ye? And they all condemned him to be guilty of death.

65 And some began to spit on him, and to cover his face, and to buffet him, and to say unto him, Prophesy: and the servants did strike him with the palms of their hands.

—MARK 14:53–65

PETER DENIES CHRIST THREE TIMES

55 And when they had kindled a fire in the midst of the hall, and were set down together, Peter sat down among them.

56 But a certain maid beheld him as he sat by the fire, and earnestly looked upon him, and said, This man was also with him.

57 And he denied him, saying, Woman, I know him not.

58 And after a little while another saw him, and said, Thou art also of them. And Peter said, Man, I am not.

59 And about the space of one hour after another confidently affirmed, saying, Of a truth this *fellow* also was with him: for he is a Galilaean.

60 And Peter said, Man, I know not what thou sayest. And immediately, while he yet spake, the cock crew.

61 And the Lord turned, and looked upon Peter. And Peter remembered the word of the Lord, how he had said unto him, Before the cock crow, thou shalt deny me thrice.

62 And Peter went out, and wept bitterly.

—LUKE 22:55–62

JUDAS COMMITS SUICIDE

1 When the morning was come, all the chief priests and elders of the people took counsel against Jesus to put him to death:

2 And when they had bound him, they led *him* away, and delivered him to Pontius Pilate the governor.

3 Then Judas, which had betrayed him, when he saw that he was condemned, repented himself, and brought again the thirty pieces of silver to the chief priests and elders,

4 Saying, I have sinned in that I have betrayed the innocent blood. And they said, What *is that* to us? see thou *to that.*

5 And he cast down the pieces of silver in the temple, and departed, and went and hanged himself.

6 And the chief priests took the silver pieces, and said, It is not lawful for to put them into the treasury, because it is the price of blood.

7 And they took counsel, and bought with them the potter's field, to bury strangers in.

8 Wherefore that field was called, The field of blood, unto this day.

9 Then was fulfilled that which was spoken by Jeremy the prophet, saying, And they took the thirty pieces of silver, the price of him that was valued, whom they of the children of Israel did value;

10 And gave them for the potter's field, as the Lord appointed me.

—MATTHEW 27:1–10

Opposite and below: Matthew tells us that when the Sanhedrin condemned Jesus to death, Judas was so overcome with remorse that he hanged himself (below) after flinging down the thirty pieces of silver, or blood money, that he had been paid for his betrayal (opposite).

CHRIST IS BROUGHT BEFORE PONTIUS PILATE

Below: After the Sanhedrin had sentenced Jesus to death for blasphemy, He was brought before Pontius Pilate on a charge of treason, His Jewish accusers telling Pilate, "We found this fellow perverting the nation, and forbidding to give tribute to Caesar, saying that he himself is Christ a King" (Luke 23:2).

11 And Jesus stood before the governor: and the governor asked him, saying, Art thou the King of the Jews? And Jesus said unto him, Thou sayest.

12 And when he was accused of the chief priests and elders, he answered nothing.

13 Then said Pilate unto him, Hearest thou not how many things they witness against thee?

14 And he answered him to never a word; insomuch that the governor marvelled greatly.

15 Now at *that* feast the governor was wont to release unto the people a prisoner, whom they would.

16 And they had then a notable prisoner, called Barabbas.

17 Therefore when they were gathered together, Pilate said unto them, Whom will ye that I release unto you? Barabbas, or Jesus which is called Christ?

18 For he knew that for envy they had delivered him.

19 When he was set down on the judgment seat, his wife sent unto him, saying, Have thou nothing to do with that just man: for I have suffered many things this day in a dream because of him.

20 But the chief priests and elders persuaded the multitude that they should ask Barabbas, and destroy Jesus.

21 The governor answered and said unto them, Whether of the twain will ye that I release unto you? They said, Barabbas.

22 Pilate saith unto them, What shall I do then with Jesus which is called Christ? *They* all say unto him, Let him be crucified.

23 And the governor said, Why, what evil hath he done? But they cried out the more, saying, Let him be crucified.

24 When Pilate saw that he could prevail nothing, but *that* rather a tumult was made, he took water, and washed

Above: Ecce homo! *After Jesus had been scourged, crowned with thorns, and garbed in a purple robe, Pilate presented Him to the chief priests and officers of the Sanhedrin with the words "Behold the man!" (John 19:5).*

Below: Pilate absolved himself symbolically of responsibility for "this just person's" death by publicly washing his hands.

his hands before the multitude, saying, I am innocent of the blood of this just person: see ye *to it*.

25 Then answered all the people, and said, His blood *be* on us, and on our children.

—MATTHEW 27:11–25

CHRIST IS
HUMILIATED

CHRIST IS SCOURGED AND MOCKED

26 Then released he Barabbas unto them: and when he had scourged Jesus, he delivered *him* to be crucified.
27 Then the soldiers of the governor took Jesus into the common hall, and gathered unto him the whole band *of soldiers.*
28 And they stripped him, and put on him a scarlet robe.
29 And when they had platted a crown of thorns, they put *it* upon his head, and a reed in his right hand: and they bowed the knee before him, and mocked him, saying, Hail, King of the Jews!

Previous page and right: Mark (15:16–20) relates that Pilate had Jesus scourged, after which his soldiers led Jesus to their hall, or praetorium, *where they called "the whole band" together to mock and humiliate Him.*

Opposite, page 52, and page 53: The Roman soldiers placed a crown of thorns on Jesus' head, then seized the reed that they had thrust into His hand to symbolize a scepter and beat Him with it, as depicted by Titian (opposite) and Caravaggio (pages 52 and 53).

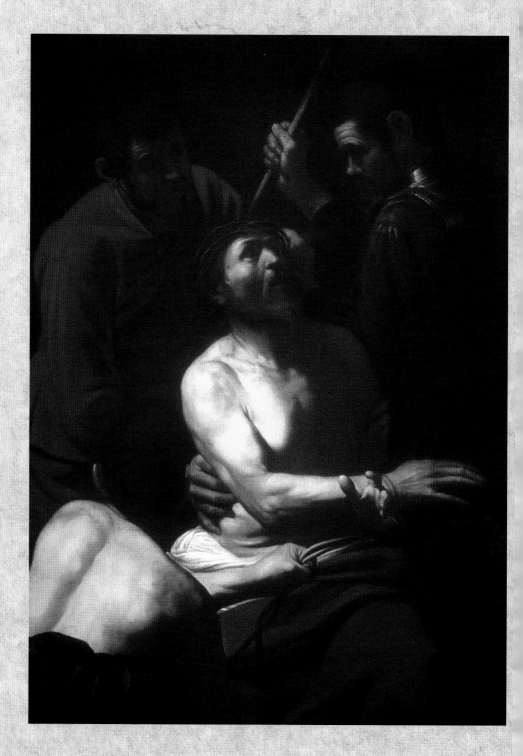

*Below: The letters on
the sign borne by the
soldier in the illustration
below stand for* Iesus
Nazarenus Rex
Iudaeorum, *the Latin
for the title* JESUS OF
NAZARETH THE KING
OF THE JEWS.

30 And they spit upon him, and took the reed, and smote
   him on the head.
31 And after that they had mocked him, they took the robe
   off from him, and put his own raiment on him, and led
   him away to crucify *him.*
32 And as they came out, they found a man of Cyrene,
   Simon by name: him they compelled to bear his cross.

—MATTHEW 27:26–32

Left: *Fra Angelico's fresco shows Christ wearing His crown of thorns and blindfolded. The artist has used a disembodied head and hands to portray Christ's humiliation symbolically rather than too graphically.*

CHRIST IS CRUCIFIED

THE CRUCIFIXION

33 And when they were come unto a place called Golgotha, that is to say, a place of a skull,

34 They gave him vinegar to drink mingled with gall: and when he had tasted *thereof*, he would not drink.

35 And they crucified him, and parted his garments, casting lots: that it might be fulfilled which was spoken by the prophet, They parted my garments among them, and upon my vesture did they cast lots.

36 And sitting down they watched him there;

37 And set up over his head his accusation written, THIS IS JESUS THE KING OF THE JEWS.

38 Then were there two thieves crucified with him, one on the right hand, and another on the left.

39 And they that passed by reviled him, wagging their heads,

40 And saying, Thou that destroyest the temple, and buildest *it* in three days, save thyself. If thou be the Son of God, come down from the cross.

41 Likewise also the chief priests mocking *him*, with the scribes and elders, said,

42 He saved others; himself he cannot save. If he be the King of Israel, let him now come down from the cross, and we will believe him.

43 He trusted in God; let him deliver him now, if he will have him: for he said, I am the Son of God.

44 The thieves also, which were crucified with him, cast the same in his teeth.

45 Now from the sixth hour there was darkness over all the land unto the ninth hour.

46 And about the ninth hour Jesus cried with a loud voice, saying, Eli, Eli, lama

Opposite: Raphael's panel shows Mary witnessing the agony endured by her son on the cross.

Below: Jesus died an excruciatingly painful death on His cross, which was placed between those of two thieves.

Below: Fra Angelico's depiction of the crucifixion.

sabachthani? that is to say, My God, my God, why hast thou forsaken me?

47 Some of them that stood there, when they heard *that*, said, This *man* calleth for Elias.

48 And straightway one of them ran, and took a spunge, and filled *it* with vinegar, and put *it* on a reed, and gave him to drink.

49 The rest said, Let be, let us see whether Elias will come to save him.

50 Jesus, when he had cried again with a loud voice, yielded up the ghost.

51 And, behold, the veil of the temple was rent in twain from the top to the bottom; and the earth did quake, and the rocks rent;

52 And the graves were opened; and many bodies of the saints which slept arose,

53 And came out of the graves after his resurrection, and went into the holy city, and appeared unto many.

54 Now when the centurion, and they that were with him, watching Jesus, saw the earthquake, and those things that were done, they feared greatly, saying, Truly this was the Son of God.

—MATTHEW 27:33–54

THE FINAL DESECRATION

31 The Jews therefore, because it was the preparation, that the bodies should not remain upon the cross on the sabbath day, (for that sabbath day was an high day,) besought Pilate that their legs might be broken, and *that* they might be taken away.

32 Then came the soldiers, and brake the legs of the first, and of the other which was crucified with him.

33 But when they came to Jesus, and saw that he was dead already, they brake not his legs:

Below: In this woodcut by Albrecht Dürer, an angel collects the blood from Jesus' pierced side (John 19:34).

34 But one of the soldiers with a spear pierced his side, and forthwith came there out blood and water.

35 And he that saw *it* bare record, and his record is true: and he knoweth that he saith true, that ye might believe.

36 For these things were done, that the scripture should be fulfilled, A bone of him shall not be broken.

37 And again another scripture saith, They shall look on him whom they pierced.

—JOHN 19:31–37

Left: *In Giotto's masterpiece* The Lamentation, *the angels and humans alike grieve for their beloved Jesus after He is deposed from the cross.*

Right: *In Raphael's
expressive painting
The Deposition (1507),
the wound in Jesus'
pierced side is clearly
visible, along with the
wounds to His hands
and feet. The distraught
Mary is faint with
grief (far right).*

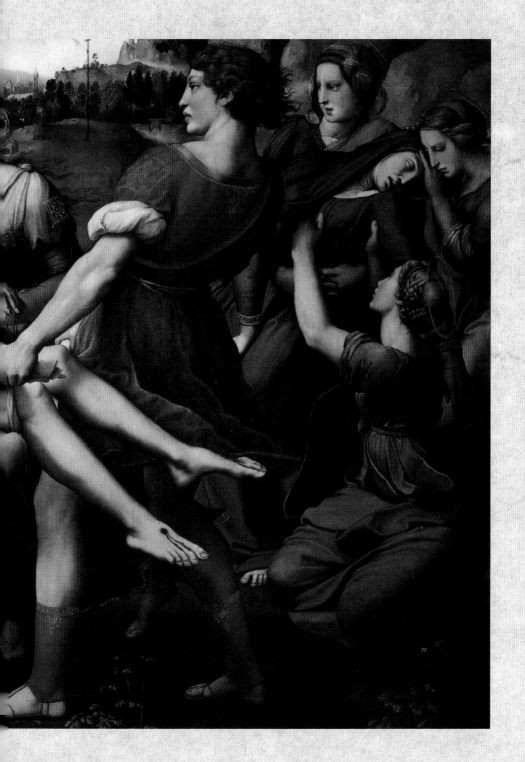

THE DEPOSITION AND ENTOMBMENT

Below, opposite, and overleaf: "Then they took the body of Jesus, and wound it in linen clothes" (John 19:40). Michelangelo, below; Caravaggio, opposite; and overleaf, Fra Angelico.

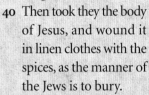

38 And after this Joseph of Arimathaea, being a disciple of Jesus, but secretly for fear of the Jews, besought Pilate that he might take away the body of Jesus: and Pilate gave *him* leave. He came therefore, and took the body of Jesus.

39 And there came also Nicodemus, which at the first came to Jesus by night, and brought a mixture of myrrh and aloes, about an hundred pound *weight*.

40 Then took they the body of Jesus, and wound it in linen clothes with the spices, as the manner of the Jews is to bury.

41 Now in the place where he was crucified there was a garden; and in the garden a new sepulchre, wherein was never man yet laid.

42 There laid they Jesus therefore because of the Jews' preparation *day*; for the sepulchre was nigh at hand.

—JOHN 19:38–42

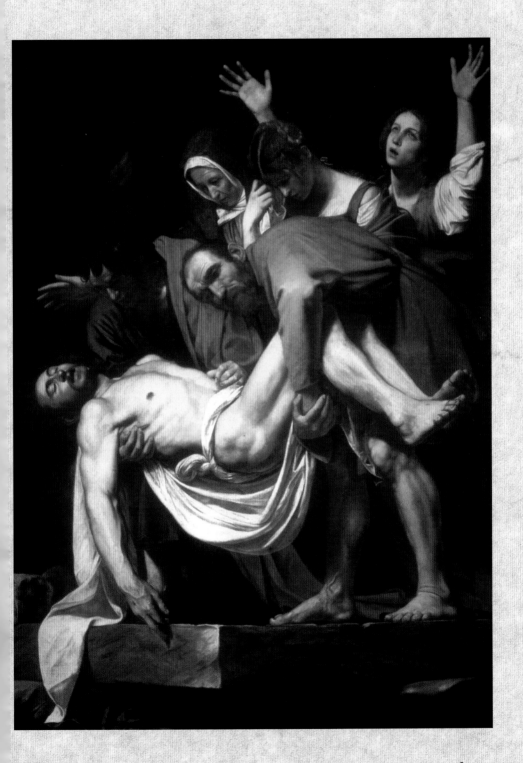

CHRIST IS RESURRECTED

THE RESURRECTION

1   Now upon the first *day* of the week, very early in the morning, they came unto the sepulchre, bringing the spices which they had prepared, and certain *others* with them.

2   And they found the stone rolled away from the sepulchre.

3   And they entered in, and found not the body of the Lord Jesus.

4   And it came to pass, as they were much perplexed thereabout, behold, two men stood by them in shining garments:

5   And as they were afraid, and bowed down their faces to the earth, they said unto them, Why seek ye the living among the dead?

6   He is not here, but is risen: remember how he spake unto you when he was yet in Galilee,

7   Saying, The Son of man must be delivered into the hands of sinful men, and be crucified, and the third day rise again.

8   And they remembered his words,

9   And returned from the sepulchre, and told all these things unto the eleven, and to all the rest.

10   It was Mary Magdalene, and Joanna, and Mary *the mother* of James, and other *women that were* with them, which told these things unto the apostles.

11   And their words seemed to them as idle tales, and they believed them not.

12   Then arose Peter, and ran unto the sepulchre; and stooping down, he beheld the linen clothes laid by themselves, and departed, wondering in himself at that which was come to pass.

—LUKE 24:1–12

Opposite: *Fra Bartolommeo (1475–1517) painted this striking portrayal of the Risen Christ.*

Below: *"He is not here, but is risen!" (Luke 24:6), the angel told Mary Magdalene at the empty tomb of Christ.*

NOLI ME TANGERE: "TOUCH ME NOT"

11 But Mary stood without at the sepulchre weeping: and as she wept, she stooped down, *and looked* into the sepulchre,

12 And seeth two angels in white sitting, the one at the head, and the other at the feet, where the body of Jesus had lain.

13 And they say unto her, Woman, why weepest thou? She saith unto them, Because they have taken away my Lord, and I know not where they have laid him.

14 And when she had thus said, she turned herself back, and saw Jesus standing, and knew not that it was Jesus.

15 Jesus saith unto her, Woman, why weepest thou? whom seekest thou? She, supposing him to be the gardener, saith unto him, Sir, if thou have borne him hence, tell me where thou hast laid him, and I will take him away.

16 Jesus saith unto her, Mary. She turned herself, and saith unto him, Rabboni; which is to say, Master.

17 Jesus saith unto her, Touch me not; for I am not yet ascended to my Father: but go to my brethren, and say unto them, I ascend unto my Father, and your Father; and *to* my God, and your God.

18 Mary Magdalene came and told the disciples that she had seen the Lord, and *that* he had spoken these things unto her.

—JOHN 20:11–18

Below: Noli Me Tangere, *by Titian (c. 1511), shows Jesus apearing to Mary Magdalene, who was the first to see the resurrected Christ.*

THE ROAD TO EMMAUS

13 And, behold, two of them went that same day to a village called Emmaus, which was from Jerusalem *about* threescore furlongs.

14 And they talked together of all these things which had happened.

15 And it came to pass, that, while they communed *together* and reasoned, Jesus himself drew near, and went with them.

16 But their eyes were holden that they should not know him.

17 And he said unto them, What manner of communications *are* these that ye have one to another, as ye walk, and are sad?

18 And the one of them, whose name was Cleopas, answering said unto him, Art thou only a stranger in Jerusalem, and hast not known the things which are come to pass there in these days?

19 And he said unto them, What things? And they said unto him, Concerning Jesus of Nazareth, which was a prophet mighty in deed and word before God and all the people:

20 And how the chief priests and our rulers delivered him to be condemned to death, and have crucified him.

21 But we trusted that it had been he which should have redeemed Israel: and beside all this, to day is the third day since these things were done.

22 Yea, and certain women also of our company made us astonished, which were early at the sepulchre;

23 And when they found not his body, they came, saying, that they had also seen a vision of angels, which said that he was alive.

Below: *This etching by Gustave Doré shows Jesus with Cleopas and his companion on the road to Emmaus.*

Below: In Titian's The Supper at Emmaus, *the resurrected Jesus reveals Himself to the astonished company as He sat with them to dine.*

24 And certain of them which were with us went to the sepulchre, and found *it* even so as the women had said: but him they saw not.

25 Then he said unto them, O fools, and slow of heart to believe all that the prophets have spoken:

26 Ought not Christ to have suffered these things, and to enter into his glory?

27 And beginning at Moses and all the prophets, he expounded unto them in all the scriptures the things concerning himself.

28 And they drew nigh unto the village, whither they went: and he made as though he would have gone further.

29 But they constrained him, saying, Abide with us: for it is toward evening, and the day is far spent. And he went in to tarry with them.

30 And it came to pass, as he sat at meat with them, he took bread, and blessed *it*, and brake, and gave to them.

31 And their eyes were opened, and they knew him; and he vanished out of their sight.

32 And they said one to another, Did not our heart burn within us, while he talked with us by the way, and while he opened to us the scriptures?

33 And they rose up the same hour, and returned to Jerusalem, and found the eleven gathered together, and them that were with them,

34 Saying, The Lord is risen indeed, and hath appeared to Simon.

35 And they told what things *were done* in the way, and how he was known of them in breaking of bread.

—LUKE 24:13–35

DOUBTING THOMAS

19 Then the same day at evening, being the first *day* of the week, when the doors were shut where the disciples were assembled for fear of the Jews, came Jesus and stood in the midst, and saith unto them, Peace *be* unto you.

20 And when he had so said, he shewed unto them his hands and his side. Then were the disciples glad, when they saw the Lord.

21 Then said Jesus to them again, Peace *be* unto you: as *my* Father hath sent me, even so send I you.

22 And when he had said this, he breathed on *them*, and saith unto them, Receive ye the Holy Ghost:

23 Whose soever sins ye remit, they are remitted unto them; *and* whose soever *sins* ye retain, they are retained.

24 But Thomas, one of the twelve, called Didymus, was not with them when Jesus came.

25 The other disciples therefore said unto him, We have seen the Lord. But he said unto them, Except I shall see

in his hands the print of the nails, and put my finger into the print of the nails, and thrust my hand into his side, I will not believe.

26 And after eight days again his disciples were within, and Thomas with them: *then* came Jesus, the doors being shut, and stood in the midst, and said, Peace *be* unto you.

27 Then saith he to Thomas, Reach hither thy finger, and behold my hands; and reach hither thy hand, and thrust *it* into my side: and be not faithless, but believing.

28 And Thomas answered and said unto him, My Lord and my God.

29 Jesus saith unto him, Thomas, because thou hast seen me, thou hast believed: blessed *are* they that have not seen, and *yet* have believed.

—JOHN 20:19–29

THE SEA OF TIBERIAS

1 After these things Jesus shewed himself again to the disciples at the sea of Tiberias; and on this wise shewed he *himself*.

2 There were together Simon Peter, and Thomas called Didymus, and Nathanael of Cana in Galilee, and the *sons* of Zebedee, and two other of his disciples.

3 Simon Peter saith unto them, I go a fishing. They say unto him, We also go with thee. They went forth, and entered into a ship immediately; and that night they caught nothing.

4 But when the morning was now come, Jesus stood on the shore: but the disciples knew not that it was Jesus.

5 Then Jesus saith unto them, Children, have ye any meat? They answered him, No.

6 And he said unto them, Cast the net on the right side of the ship, and ye shall find. They cast therefore, and now they were not able to draw it for the multitude of fishes.

7 Therefore that disciple whom Jesus loved saith unto Peter, It is the Lord. Now when Simon Peter heard that it was the Lord, he girt *his* fisher's coat *unto him*, (for he was naked,) and did cast himself into the sea.

8 And the other disciples came in a little ship; (for they were not far from land, but as it were two hundred cubits,) dragging the net with fishes.

9 As soon then as they were come to land, they saw a fire of coals there, and fish laid thereon, and bread.

10 Jesus saith unto them, Bring of the fish which ye have now caught.

11 Simon Peter went up, and drew the net to land full of great fishes, an hundred and fifty and three: and for all there were so many, yet was not the net broken.

12 Jesus saith unto them, Come *and* dine. And none of the disciples durst ask him, Who art thou? knowing that it was the Lord.

13 Jesus then cometh, and taketh bread, and giveth them, and fish likewise.

14 This is now the third time that Jesus shewed himself to his disciples, after that he was risen from the dead.

15 So when they had dined, Jesus saith to Simon Peter, Simon, *son* of Jonas, lovest thou me more than these? He saith unto him, Yea, Lord; thou knowest that I love thee. He saith unto him, Feed my lambs.

16 He saith to him again the second time, Simon, *son* of Jonas, lovest thou me? He saith unto him, Yea, Lord; thou knowest that I love thee. He saith unto him, Feed my sheep.

Above: Christ revealed Himself to the disciples for the third time, in a scene depicted here by Raphael (1515), The Miraculous Draught of Fishes.

17 He saith unto him the third time, Simon, *son* of Jonas, lovest thou me? Peter was grieved because he said unto him the third time, Lovest thou me? And he said unto him, Lord, thou knowest all things; thou knowest that I love thee. Jesus saith unto him, Feed my sheep.

18 Verily, verily, I say unto thee, When thou wast young, thou girdest thyself, and walkedst whither thou wouldest: but when thou shalt be old, thou shalt stretch forth thy hands, and another shall gird thee, and carry *thee* whither thou wouldest not.

19 This spake he, signifying by what death he should glorify God. And when he had spoken this, he saith unto him, Follow me.

20 Then Peter, turning about, seeth the disciple whom Jesus loved following; which also leaned on his breast at supper, and said, Lord, which is he that betrayeth thee?

21 Peter seeing him saith to Jesus, Lord, and what *shall* this man *do*?

22 Jesus saith unto him, If I will that he tarry till I come, what *is that* to thee? follow thou me.

23 Then went this saying abroad among the brethren, that that disciple should not die: yet Jesus said not unto him, He shall not die; but, If I will that he tarry till I come, what *is that* to thee?

24 This is the disciple which testifieth of these things, and wrote these things: and we know that his testimony is true.

—JOHN 21:1–24

CHRIST ASCENDS INTO HEAVEN

45 Then opened he their understanding, that they might understand the scriptures,

46 And said unto them, Thus it is written, and thus it behoved Christ to suffer, and to rise from the dead the third day:

47 And that repentance and remission of sins should be preached in his name among all nations, beginning at Jerusalem.

48 And ye are witnesses of these things.

49 And, behold, I send the promise of my Father upon you: but tarry ye in the city of Jerusalem, until ye be endued with power from on high.

50 And he led them out as far as to Bethany, and he lifted up his hands, and blessed them.

51 And it came to pass, while he blessed them, he was parted from them, and carried up into heaven.

52 And they worshipped him, and returned to Jerusalem with great joy:

53 And were continually in the temple, praising and bless-ing God. Amen.

Above and overleaf:
After appearing to the disciples for the last time (above: Bellini's Transformation of Christ*), Jesus ascended to Heaven on the third day (page 79: Raphael's* The Transfiguration*).*

—LUKE 24:45–53

INDEX

Page numbers in *italics*
refer to illustrations.

The Wisdom of the
PARABLES

The Wisdom of the PARABLES

ROBIN LANGLEY SOMMER

Saraband

Page 1: *Christ with the cross, by Michelangelo.*

Page 2: *Jesus taught His principles by relating them in stories of everyday situations.*

Page 3: *A detail from a painting by Hieronymus Bosch, which recalls Christ as the shepherd.*

Published by Saraband (Scotland) Limited,
The Arthouse, 752–756 Argyle Street,
Glasgow G3 8UJ, Scotland
hermes@saraband.net

ISBN: 1-887354-17-4

Printed in China

10 9 8 7 6 5 4 3 2

Acknowledgements
Extracts from the Authorized Version of the Bible (The King James Bible), the rights in which are vested in the Crown, are reproduced by permission of the Crown's Patentee, Cambridge University Press.

The publisher would like to thank the following people for their assistance in the preparation of this book: Debbie Hayes, Sara Hunt, Phoebe Wong, Nicola Gillies, and Wendy J. Ciaccia Eurell. Grateful acknowledgement is also made for the illustrations featured in this book, which are reproduced by courtesy of Planet Art, 2002 Arttoday.com, Inc., and CorelDraw, except those on pages 15, 30, 41, 43, 64 and 77, which are courtesy of Saraband Image Library.

This book is dedicated to the memory of Reverend Canon Leonard A. Cragg

Contents

INTRODUCTION

The word "parable," derived from the Greek *parabolé* (comparison), describes a brief allegorical story that conveys a moral lesson, spiritual principle, or universal truth. There was a long tradition of parabolic teaching in the East when Christ undertook His teaching ministry, but the stories He told have lived for 2,000 years. At the heart of them are everyday events like a woman searching for a lost coin, a farmer concerned about the weeds in his grain field and a father welcoming his son home. But underlying their apparent simplicity is a power that conveys truth to anyone who seeks it, because these tales were told by Christ and bear the unmistakable stamp of His personality and of the radical message He brought. As Scripture scholar C.W.F. Smith observed in *The Jesus of the Parables* (1948): "[Here] Jesus appears as no Eastern sage or objective moralist, but as the Initiator of God's new age and the Agent of His purpose. He is not [only] the kindly advocate of brotherly love, but the revealer of the dreadful love of God and the awe of the divine mercy."

Christ drew upon the rabbinic parables when he told the stories that left an indelible impression upon people's minds. The Evangelists wrote that "the people were astonished at His doctrine; for He taught as one having authority, and not as the scribes" (Matthew 7:28–29). Luke tells us that He spent three days in the Temple at the age of twelve, "sitting in the midst of the doctors, both hearing them, and asking them questions. And all that heard him were astonished at his understanding and answers" (2: 46–47).

The parables of Christ added a new dimension to the oral and written tradition of the Hebrews. One aspect of it was a deep empathy with the natural world, as seen in the parables of the Mustard Seed, the Budding Fig Tree, the Lost Sheep, the Lilies of the Field and many others. Throughout the Gospels Christ expressed a love for the animal creation that was unparalleled in antiquity. His teachings are filled with images from nature that show compassion for all creatures and intuitive knowledge of their ways. Animals are often used as images of spirituality as contrasted with worldliness. When Christ mourned over Jerusalem, He compared Himself to a hen that wanted to shelter her chicks under her wings to protect them from danger (Matthew 23:37). He saw the shepherd, the sower and the vinedresser as people in touch with God through their affinity with the natural world.

Christ also showed profound insight into the best (and worst) in human nature. He taught that every person had equal value in the eyes of God and must be treated accordingly. His bias was toward the poor and afflicted, whom the world considered no one, but His invitation was to all. The many parables of grace and of the Kingdom call for human effort and co-operation, but their primary emphasis is on the loving initiative of God in establishing divine order in all relationships. The parables of the Good Samaritan, the Prodigal Son and the Good Shepherd pushed far beyond the boundaries previously set by every religion between God and humankind. Christ was the first to call God "Father." This concept was radically new, unheard of until His coming. It shifted the whole basis of morality from crude human ideas of justice to the immeasurable mercy of God as manifested in Christ. To this day, the parables serve as an open door to those who first asked 2,000 years ago: "We should like to see Jesus" (John 12:21).

ON FAITH

On Faith

Previous page: A Renaissance painting by Bellini shows Christ transfigured between the prophets Moses and Elijah before His wondering disciples.

Among the best-known parables on faith are those of the Hidden Treasure and the Pearl of Great Price. They may have been told together, or grouped together later, as parallelism is characteristic of Hebrew style. Other examples of twin parables include the Mustard Seed and the Leaven and the Houses Built on Sand and on Rock.

The theme common to the Hidden Treasure and the Pearl of Great Price is the joy of attainment. In the first parable, the treasure is found by accident—perhaps buried for safekeeping by a wealthy person in time of war. The fortunate man who comes upon it while he is digging sells all that he has to buy the field and make the treasure his own. The merchant, on the other hand, has spent his life buying and selling pearls. He knows their worth, and is vigilant about finding the peerless pearl. When he does so, he invests all he has to acquire the pearl of great price. In his case, the finding of the pearl is the result of long and deliberate seeking, but both he and the farmer, whose find far exceeded his hopes, achieve the same gifts of grace.

The importance of a sound foundation is expressed in the parallel of the Two Builders. Christ draws a contrast between hearing and then acting according to His teachings, and hearing without taking action. The man who builds his house on a stone foundation will not be swept away when temptations and trials assault him, but the person who builds upon sand—perhaps in one of the *wadis* subject to periodic flooding in the Middle East—will see his house collapse. This example of the difference between hearing and doing has an antecedent in the Book of Proverbs (10:25), which reads: "When the whirlwind passeth, the wicked is no more: But the righteous is an everlasting foundation."

The parable of the Mustard Seed speaks to the concepts of enlargement and shelter through faith, while that of the Leaven emphasizes the idea of transformation. The tiny size of the "grain of mustard"—metaphorically, the initial act of faith—is contrasted with that of the mature "tree" (actually a large bush, some eight to ten feet tall), which offers shelter to the birds that alight on its branches. Like its counterpart, the parable of the small amount of leaven or yeast that can activate a great mass of dough, this parable foresees the extension and growth from small beginnings of the Kingdom, which offers both shelter and nourishment to all who are drawn to it, including the Gentiles.

The twin parables of the Patch and the Wineskins have sometimes been interpreted as a statement of incompatibility between Judaism and Christianity. However, this ignores the fact that Christ repeatedly stated that he had come to complete the Old Law, not to abolish it. It was an axiom that patching an old garment with new (unshrunk) cloth would only make the tear worse. Likewise, everyone knew that new wine poured into old wineskins would burst them. What is implied here may not be incompatibility, but a creative synthesis, such as that made explicit in Matthew's parable of the householder whose treasure is of greater value because it consists of both new and old elements (13:52). It is possible that these three stories were told together but transcribed separately.

One of the many beautiful parables from nature is that of the Sower, whose seed stands for the teaching that will yield an abundant harvest for the Kingdom of God. At the same time, the seed represents the listeners, who must undergo a process of growth and maturation. Each of those who first heard this parable could identify with the adversities faced by the sower— marauding birds, scorching sun, careless people treading

Below: The farmer, as depicted here by Van Gogh, figures in many of the Gospel parables, which were addressed mainly to the country people of Israel.

down the seedlings, weeds springing up. Each new problem called for a hopeful response based on the conviction that the harvest was certain despite human frailties, because God's purpose could not be thwarted. This parable combines realistic warnings about the difficulties faced in pursuing the life of the spirit with encouragement that failures and trials can be instrumental to spiritual growth, and that faith through adversity brings deeper spiritual values.

In the Unjust Judge, we find a parable of grace that contrasts the behavior of the unjust judge with that of God. The judge is defined as a hard-hearted, corrupt official who "cared nothing for God or man." The only reason he finally gives in to the widow's pleas for justice is that she has worn him out. His behavior is not to be admired; rather, he seeks his own self-interest even in doing the right thing. All through the Bible, the widow represents those who need aid and compassion. Here she stands for everyone who asks for help urgently in prayer, and unlike the judge, God is moved by her urgency and responds in kind. The lesson of this parable is "how much more" God will hear the prayers of His people and do them justice.

According to Matthew, the parable of the Sheep and the Goats was the last one spoken by Christ before His passion and death. It looks forward to the end of time and prophesies His second coming in glory to reward the just and segregate those who still have to learn the meaning of mercy. The contrast between the sheep at the king's right hand—a symbol of divine favor and authority—and the goats, whose false pride has distanced them from God and others, is a stark one. Neither "saints" nor "sinners" are fully aware that their compassion, or lack of it, is the criterion whereby they have, in fact, judged themselves. But Christ makes this unmistakably clear when he says, "Inasmuch as ye have done it unto one of the least of these my brethren, ye have done it unto me." Thus Christ proclaims both His solidarity with all people through the Incarnation and the fulfillment of the new law of love in His person. This teaching has been variously described as: the Mystical Body of Christ, encompassing all creation; the Shekinah, or manifestation of Divine Presence; and the Great Spirit, source and sustainer of all that is. The message is clear, no matter how one defines it. Unconditional love and compassion draw us closer to God as we understand God.

Grace is the theme of the parable often called the Importunate Friend. Like the unjust judge, the drowsy householder first refuses his neighbor's urgent request, not because of ill will, but because it is inconvenient for him to get up and answer the door. However, the neighbor's persistence carries the day. He throws himself upon the mercy of his friend quite shamelessly, pressing his request for three loaves of bread to feed the hungry visitor who has arrived unexpectedly in the middle of the night. He makes no pretense of being a good neighbor, a good host or a good anything. His need is his only claim on the sleepy householder, who finally gets up and gives him what he asks for. This parable speaks to our utter reliance upon the mercy rather than the justice of God, to grace as a gift offered freely to all rather than a merit badge handed out to a select few for observing all the rules.

Below: The afflicted Christ on the Way of the Cross, from a medieval Book of Hours.

THE HIDDEN TREASURE AND THE PEARL OF GREAT PRICE

44 Again, the kingdom of heaven is like unto treasure hid in a field; the which when a man hath found, he hideth, and for joy thereof goeth and selleth all that he hath, and buyeth that field.

45 Again, the kingdom of heaven is like unto a merchant man, seeking goodly pearls:

46 Who, when he had found one pearl of great price, went and sold all that he had, and bought it.

—MATTHEW 13:44–46

Above: *In the parable of the Pearl of Great Price, Jesus taught that the kingdom of Heaven is worth more than everything we have.*

HOUSES BUILT ON ROCK AND SAND

47 Whosoever cometh to me, and heareth my sayings, and doeth them, I will shew you to whom he is like:

48 He is like a man which built an house, and digged deep, and laid the foundation on a rock: and when the flood arose, the stream beat vehemently upon that house, and could not shake it: for it was founded upon a rock.

49 But he that heareth, and doeth not, is like a man that without a foundation built an house upon the earth; against which the stream did beat vehemently, and immediately it fell; and the ruin of that house was great.

—LUKE 6:47–49

THE MUSTARD SEED AND THE LEAVEN

31 Another parable put he forth unto them, saying, The kingdom of heaven is like to a grain of mustard seed, which a man took, and sowed in his field:

32 Which indeed is the least of all seeds: but when it is grown, it is the greatest among herbs, and becometh a tree, so that the birds of the air come and lodge in the branches thereof.

33 Another parable spake he unto them; The kingdom of heaven is like unto leaven, which a woman took, and hid in three measures of meal, till the whole was leavened.

—MATTHEW 13:31–33

Left: A woman kneads bread dough containing the leaven (yeast) that will make it rise into a wholesome loaf.

NEW CLOTH ON OLD GARMENTS; NEW WINE IN OLD BOTTLES

Below: *This pastoral scene by Van Gogh,* Wheatfield with Poppies and Lark, *recalls the lesson embodied in the parable of the Sower when the seeds had fallen on fertile ground and flourished.*

36 And he spake also a parable unto them; No man putteth a piece of a new garment upon an old; if otherwise, then both the new maketh a rent, and the piece that was *taken* out of the new agreeth not with the old.

37 And no man putteth new wine into old bottles; else the new wine will burst the bottles, and be spilled, and the bottles shall perish.

38 But new wine must be put into new bottles; and both are preserved.

—LUKE 5:36–38

THE SOWER

1   And he began again to teach by the sea side: and there was gathered unto him a great multitude, so that he entered into a ship, and sat in the sea; and the whole multitude was by the sea on the land.

2   And he taught them many things by parables, and said unto them in his doctrine,

3   Hearken; Behold, there went out a sower to sow:

4   And it came to pass, as he sowed, some fell by the way side, and the fowls of the air came and devoured it up.

5   And some fell on stony ground, where it had not much earth; and immediately it sprang up, because it had no depth of earth:

6   But when the sun was up, it was scorched; and because it had no root, it withered away.

7   And some fell among thorns, and the thorns grew up, and choked it, and it yielded no fruit.

8   And other fell on good ground, and did yield fruit that sprang up and increased; and brought forth, some thirty, and some sixty, and some an hundred.

9   And he said unto them, He that hath ears to hear, let him hear.

10 And when he was alone, they that were about him with the twelve asked of him the parable.

11 And he said unto them, Unto you it is given to know the mystery of the kingdom of God: but unto them that are without, all *these* things are done in parables:

12 That seeing they may see, and not perceive; and hearing they may hear, and not understand; lest at any time they should be converted, and *their* sins should be forgiven them.

13 And he said unto them, Know ye not this parable? and how then will ye know all parables?

14 The sower soweth the word.

15 And these are they by the way side, where the word is sown; but when they have heard, Satan cometh imme-

diately, and taketh away the word that was sown in their hearts.

16 And these are they likewise which are sown on stony ground; who, when they have heard the word, immediately receive it with gladness;

17 And have no root in themselves, and so endure but for a time: afterward, when affliction or persecution ariseth for the word's sake, immediately they are offended.

18 And these are they which are sown among thorns; such as hear the word,

19 And the cares of this world, and the deceitfulness of riches, and the lusts of other things entering in, choke the word, and it becometh unfruitful.

20 And these are they which are sown on good ground; such as hear the word, and receive *it*, and bring forth fruit, some thirtyfold, some sixty, and some an hundred.

—MARK 4:1–20

Below: The diligent sower who has worked hard to overcome all the dangers that threatened his or her crop is rewarded by a bountiful harvest.

THE UNJUST JUDGE

1 And he spake a parable unto them *to this end*, that men ought always to pray, and not to faint;

2 Saying, There was in a city a judge, which feared not God, neither regarded man:

3 And there was a widow in that city; and she came unto him, saying, Avenge me of mine adversary.

4 And he would not for a while: but afterward he said within himself, Though I fear not God, nor regard man;

5 Yet because this widow troubleth me, I will avenge her, lest by her continual coming she weary me.

6 And the Lord said, Hear what the unjust judge saith.

7 And shall not God avenge his own elect, which cry day and night unto him, though he bear long with them?

8 I tell you that he will avenge them speedily. Nevertheless when the Son of man cometh, shall he find faith on the earth?

—LUKE 18:1–8

Below: In the foreground of this Fra Angelico fresco are three of the Apostles, who were among the first to demonstrate their faith in Christ as the prophesied savior.

THE SHEEP AND THE GOATS

31 When the Son of man shall come in his glory, and all the holy angels with him, then shall he sit upon the throne of his glory:

32 And before him shall be gathered all nations: and he shall separate them one from another, as a shepherd divideth *his* sheep from the goats:

33 And he shall set the sheep on his right hand, but the goats on the left.

34 Then shall the King say unto them on his right hand, Come, ye blessed of my Father, inherit the kingdom prepared for you from the foundation of the world:

35 For I was an hungred, and ye gave me meat: I was thirsty, and ye gave me drink: I was a stranger, and ye took me in:

36 Naked, and ye clothed me: I was sick, and ye visited me: I was in prison, and ye came unto me.

37 Then shall the righteous answer him, saying, Lord, when saw we thee an hungred, and fed *thee*? or thirsty, and gave *thee* drink?

38 When saw we thee a stranger, and took *thee* in? or naked, and clothed *thee*?

39 Or when saw we thee sick, or in prison, and came unto thee?

40 And the King shall answer and say unto them, Verily I say unto you, Inasmuch as ye have done *it* unto one of the least of these my brethren, ye have done *it* unto me.

41 Then shall he say also unto them on the left hand, Depart from me, ye cursed, into everlasting fire, prepared for the devil and his angels:

42 For I was an hungred, and ye gave me no meat: I was thirsty, and ye gave me no drink:

43 I was a stranger, and ye took me not in: naked, and ye clothed me not: sick, and in prison, and ye visited me not.

44 Then shall they also answer him, saying, Lord, when saw we thee an hungred, or athirst, or a stranger, or naked,

or sick, or in prison, and did not minister unto thee?
45 Then shall he answer them, saying, Verily I say unto you,
Inasmuch as ye did *it* not to one of the least of these, ye
did *it* not to me.
46 And these shall go away into everlasting punishment:
but the righteous into life eternal.

—MATTHEW 25:31–46

Left: *Giotto's awe-inspiring vision of the Last Judgement, featuring the Risen Christ. In this parable, Jesus describes how each of us will be judged by our own actions.*

THE IMPORTUNATE FRIEND

5   And he said unto them, Which of you shall have a friend, and shall go unto him at midnight, and say unto him, Friend, lend me three loaves;

6   For a friend of mine in his journey is come to me, and I have nothing to set before him?

7   And he from within shall answer and say, Trouble me not: the door is now shut, and my children are with me in bed; I cannot rise and give thee.

8   I say unto you, Though he will not rise and give him, because he is his friend, yet because of his importunity he will rise and give him as many as he needeth.

—LUKE 11:5–8

Right: Rembrandt's Head of Christ *(1650) is a moving portrait of the teller of this parable that encourages perseverance in prayer. Conversely, Christ is also "the importunate friend" who seeks to awaken us to our spiritual identity as children of God.*

ON
RELATIONSHIPS

On Relationships

Previous page: In this masterful painting, Hieronymus Bosch portrayed the Prodigal Son looking back with contrition at his past mistakes as he heads home, hoping to redeem himself.

All of the parables on relationships described here have two levels of meaning, based on the new model of Christ as exemplar of both the fully human and the divine. They show that it is the humble and the outcasts who are most receptive to His teachings on grace as against judgement, in relationships with God and with one another.

In the story of the Two Sons whose father asks them to work in the vineyard, the first refuses to go, and the second answers with a facile "Yes, sir," but does not obey. Meanwhile, the first son realizes that he has offended his father by his refusal and changes his mind. In the end, it is he who goes into the vineyard to do a day's work. Christ compares the two brothers to those who responded to John the Baptist's call for repentance and those who ignored it, respectively. He tells his hearers that "the publicans [the despised Roman tax collectors] and the harlots believed him: and ye, when ye had seen it, repented not afterward, that ye might believe him."

This parable is analogous to that of the Pharisee and the Publican, usually cited as an example of humility commended by Christ versus smug self-righteousness. Both these men were at prayer, the Pharisee giving thanks that he wasn't sinful like the tax collector over there (the Publican) who, in turn, was "standing afar off" with downcast eyes praying, "God be merciful to me a sinner." In fact, *neither* of them has a legitimate claim on God's grace, but the Publican knows it, while the Pharisee is still picking through the rummage bag of his supposed good works to justify himself. As theologian Robert Farrar Capon puts it in his provocative book *The Parables of Grace* (Eerdmans, 1988): "We all long to establish our identity by seeing ourselves as approved in other people's eyes." Therefore, he continues, we concern ourselves with appearances rather than true values, and we are consequently afraid of exposure. However, we cannot hide our true natures from God, and we should work to build loving relationships instead of distancing ourselves through false barriers.

Another well-known parable is that of the Good Samaritan, who goes out of his way to help a Jewish man assaulted by robbers and left for dead. There had been intense antipathy between the Jews and the Samaritans on religious grounds since the conquest and repopulation of Samaria, part of Israel's Northern Kingdom, by Assyria in 721 BC. Thus, the Biblical command to "Love thy neighbour as thyself" (Lev. 19:18) was not construed by Christ's audience as extending to the Samaritans. The Jews sought to limit the definition of "neighbour" to fellow members of their faith community. Christ turned this idea on its head by showing the lengths to which the Samaritan went in rescuing the unfortunate wounded man, who had been ignored by both a priest and a Levite. In fact, he risked his own life by lifting the injured man onto his beast of burden to carry him to the next town. The seventeen-mile road between Jerusalem and Jericho was a haunt of bandits, where violence was so frequent that historian Josephus called this route "the Ascent of Blood." In this parable, Christ preaches a revolutionary doctrine

Below: Originally an expression of abhorrence, "Samaritan" came to represent Christian charity and goodwill through the teachings of Jesus. Here, the Samaritan stops to help the wounded man.

of unbounded compassion flowing from each person's inestimable value in the eyes of God. The touchstone of this unique value for the Christian is the fact that Christ died for all on the "ascent of blood" to Calvary.

The universal offer of salvation recurs in the parable of the Wedding Feast, a retelling of a traditional rabbinic parable. The king who prepared a feast for his son's marriage first invited those who could be

considered fit to attend, but all of them made excuses and refused the invitation. Angered, he told his servants to invite new guests, so they "gathered together all as many as they found, both bad and good: and the wedding was furnished with guests." The king approved all who had come except for a single guest who did not have on a clean garment (symbolic of repentance). He was excluded from the feast, as in the original version found in the Babylonian Talmud, which concludes: "Let those who have adorned themselves for the feast sit and eat and drink; but as for those who have not adorned themselves..., they shall stand and look on."

One of the most telling parables on relationships is the story of the Unmerciful Servant. He owed his master an immense debt—10,000 talents (a quantity of gold or silver)—and was about to be sold into slavery with his whole family when he begged for mercy and promised to pay all that he owed. His master "was moved with compassion and loosed him, and forgave him the debt." But rather than follow his master's example, the unmerciful servant went out to a fellow servant who owed him a small sum, seized him and throttled him, demanding, "Pay me that thou owest." Ignoring the debtor's pleas for patience, the unmerciful servant had him thrown into prison. When their master heard of it, he was extremely angry and had the hard-hearted servant punished severely. Lest anyone should miss the point of this story, Christ made it explicit: "So likewise shall my heavenly Father do also unto you, if ye from your hearts forgive not every one his brother their trespasses."

The parable of the Lost Sheep has touched human hearts for almost 2,000 years. Here the tragedy of desolation—of being cut off from one's community—is redressed by a seeking God, in the person of the shepherd, who will not rest until he has found the strayed member of his flock. Sheep are highly social animals, and one that has strayed is nearly helpless unless it can attach itself to a familiar human being. For this reason, the shepherd has to carry the bewildered animal back to the flock "on his shoulders." The emphasis on the joy of the shepherd and his friends over the recovery of the lost sheep reflects the "joy [that] shall be in heaven over one sinner that repenteth, more than over ninety and nine just persons, which need no repentance."

This theme deepens in the parable of the Prodigal Son, who left his family after demanding his inheritance "and took his journey into a far country, and there wasted his substance in riotous living." Here, instead of a sheep, we have a man, the most social of all animals, and he has strayed not across a hillside, but into a "far country," where he faces famine and destitution. His lostness is devastating, because he feels cut off from both God and his fellow men. At last, he has a change of heart and resolves to go home as a servant, if his father will have him back. But even as he thinks over his plea to be taken in as a servant, "no more worthy to be called thy son," his father sees him approach and hastens out to embrace him, scarcely heeding his apology in his joy to have him back. The whole household is called upon to prepare a feast and celebrate the prodigal's return. When the responsible elder

Below: *Both the lion and the king are emblems of Christ in His majesty and strength, as seen in this medieval illustration from a Book of Hours.*

brother comes in from the fields, he is affronted, but his father entreats him to join the celebration, "for this thy brother was dead, and is alive again; and was lost, and is found." Perhaps never before had Christ's Jewish audience heard so strong a statement of God's love for them. It echoes in the human heart to this day, making the story of the Prodigal Son one of the best-loved parables of all.

The story of the Two Debtors is another parable of forgiveness, which contrasts with that of the Unmerciful Servant. Each of the Two Debtors was forgiven his debt by a compassionate creditor, but one had owed far more than the other. Christ poses the question, "which of them will love him [the creditor] most?" The Pharisee Simon replies, "I suppose that *he*, to whom he forgave most," and this judgement is approved by Christ. The story implies that love, which is of God, covers a multitude of sins, and forgiveness is one of its signs. The Unmerciful Servant, by contrast, is depicted as a lost soul, because he can neither receive nor give love, while each of the Two Debtors returns love in proportion to the kindness he has received.

Faithfulness to stewardship of God's gifts is the theme of the Wise Steward, whose responsible behavior in his master's absence is compared to that of the servant who proves unfaithful. According to clergyman Edward A. Armstrong, an authority on folklore and author of *The Gospel Parables* (Sheed and Ward, 1967): "It is possible that [this] parable has been coloured by what happened to Nadan in the Story of Ahikar, preserved in many languages and introduced into the *One Thousand and One Nights*. The Aramaic version dates from the fifth century BC. Believing his uncle, the King of Assyria, to be dead, Nadan gathers 'vain and lewd folk' to a feast and strips and whips the menservants and handmaidens. He is found out and flogged; whereupon he swells up and bursts asunder." This would account for the uncharacteristically violent punishment described in Luke's account—"cut him in sunder"—which is generally attributed to a mistranslation from the Aramaic.

THE TWO SONS

28 But what think ye? A *certain* man had two sons; and he came to the first, and said, Son, go work to day in my vineyard.

29 He answered and said, I will not: but afterward he repented, and went.

30 And he came to the second, and said likewise. And he answered and said, I *go*, sir: and went not.

31 Whether of them twain did the will of *his* father? They say unto him, The first. Jesus saith unto them, Verily I say unto you, That the publicans and the harlots go into the kingdom of God before you.

32 For John came unto you in the way of righteousness, and ye believed him not: but the publicans and the harlots believed him: and ye, when ye had seen *it*, repented not afterward, that ye might believe him.

—MATTHEW 21:28–32

Below: A portrait by Hieronymus Bosch of John the Baptist, whom Christ called the greatest of all the prophets. The poor and the outcast heard his message of repentance most clearly and acted upon it.

THE PHARISEE AND THE PUBLICAN

9 And he spake this parable unto certain which trusted in themselves that they were righteous, and despised others:

10 Two men went up into the temple to pray; the one a Pharisee, and the other a publican.

11 The Pharisee stood and prayed thus with himself, God, I thank thee, that I am not as other men *are*, extortioners, unjust, adulterers, or even as this publican.

12 I fast twice in the week, I give tithes of all that I possess.

13 And the publican, standing afar off, would not lift up so much as *his* eyes unto heaven, but smote upon his breast, saying, God be merciful to me a sinner.

14 I tell you, this man went down to his house justified *rather* than the other: for every one that exalteth himself shall be abased; and he that humbleth himself shall be exalted.

—LUKE 18:9–14

Below: The humility of the publican (left) was more acceptable to God than the self-righteousness of the Pharisee, who prided himself on fulfilling all the prescriptions of the Old Law.

THE GOOD SAMARITAN

30 And Jesus answering said, A certain *man* went down from Jerusalem to Jericho, and fell among thieves, which stripped him of his raiment, and wounded *him*, and departed, leaving *him* half dead.

31 And by chance there came down a certain priest that way: and when he saw him, he passed by on the other side.

32 And likewise a Levite, when he was at the place, came and looked *on him*, and passed by on the other side.

33 But a certain Samaritan, as he journeyed, came where he was: and when he saw him, he had compassion *on him*,

34 And went to *him*, and bound up his wounds, pouring in oil and wine, and set him on his own beast, and brought him to an inn, and took care of him.

35 And on the morrow when he departed, he took out two pence, and gave *them* to the host, and said unto him, Take care of him; and whatsoever thou spendest more, when I come again, I will repay thee.

36 Which now of these three, thinkest thou, was neighbour unto him that fell among the thieves?

37 And he said, He that shewed mercy on him. Then said Jesus unto him, Go, and do thou likewise.

—LUKE 10:30–37

Below: In this engraving, the Good Samaritan lifts the wounded traveler from his horse so he can take care of him at a nearby inn. Through this parable, his actions became a byword for selfless compassion.

THE MARRIAGE FEAST

Opposite: There are several stories in the life of Christ that are based on marriage feasts. The parables were lessons taught by describing events or people in familiar contexts.

2 The kingdom of heaven is like unto a certain king, which made a marriage for his son,

3 And sent forth his servants to call them that were bidden to the wedding: and they would not come.

4 Again, he sent forth other servants, saying, Tell them which are bidden, Behold, I have prepared my dinner: my oxen and *my* fatlings *are* killed, and all things *are* ready: come unto the marriage.

5 But they made light of *it*, and went their ways, one to his farm, another to his merchandise:

6 And the remnant took his servants, and entreated *them* spitefully, and slew *them*.

7 But when the king heard *thereof*, he was wroth: and he sent forth his armies, and destroyed those murderers, and burned up their city.

8 Then saith he to his servants, The wedding is ready, but they which were bidden were not worthy.

9 Go ye therefore into the highways, and as many as ye shall find, bid to the marriage.

10 So those servants went out into the highways, and gathered together all as many as they found, both bad and good: and the wedding was furnished with guests.

11 And when the king came in to see the guests, he saw there a man which had not on a wedding garment:

12 And he saith unto him, Friend, how camest thou in hither not having a wedding garment? And he was speechless.

13 Then said the king to the servants, Bind him hand and foot, and take him away, and cast *him* into outer darkness; there shall be weeping and gnashing of teeth.

14 For many are called, but few *are* chosen.

—MATTHEW 22:2–14

THE UNMERCIFUL SERVANT

23 Therefore is the kingdom of heaven likened unto a certain king, which would take account of his servants.

24 And when he had begun to reckon, one was brought unto him, which owed him ten thousand talents.

25 But forasmuch as he had not to pay, his lord commanded him to be sold, and his wife, and children, and all that he had, and payment to be made.

26 The servant therefore fell down, and worshipped him, saying, Lord, have patience with me, and I will pay thee all.

27 Then the lord of that servant was moved with compassion, and loosed him, and forgave him the debt.

28 But the same servant went out, and found one of his fellowservants, which owed him an hundred pence: and he laid hands on him, and took *him* by the throat, saying, Pay me that thou owest.

29 And his fellowservant fell down at his feet, and besought him, saying, Have patience with me, and I will pay thee all.

30 And he would not: but went and cast him into prison, till he should pay the debt.

31 So when his fellowservants saw what was done, they were very sorry, and came and told unto their lord all that was done.

32 Then his lord, after that he had called him, said unto him, O thou wicked servant, I forgave thee all that debt, because thou desiredst me:

33 Shouldest not thou also have had compassion on thy fellowservant, even as I had pity on thee?

34 And his lord was wroth, and delivered him to the tormentors, till he should pay all that was due unto him.

35 So likewise shall my heavenly Father do also unto you, if ye from your hearts forgive not every one his brother their trespasses.

—MATTHEW 18:23–35

THE LOST SHEEP

3 And he spake this parable unto them, saying,

4 What man of you, having an hundred sheep, if he lose one of them, doth not leave the ninety and nine in the wilderness, and go after that which is lost, until he find it?

5 And when he hath found *it*, he layeth *it* on his shoulders, rejoicing.

6 And when he cometh home, he calleth together *his* friends and neighbours, saying unto them, Rejoice with me; for I have found my sheep which was lost.

7 I say unto you, that likewise joy shall be in heaven over one sinner that repenteth, more than over ninety and nine just persons, which need no repentance.

—LUKE 15:3–7

Below: *A medieval artist was inspired by the parable of the Lost Sheep to depict the well-loved story in his own milieu for a Book of Hours.*

The Prodigal Son

11 And he said, A certain man had two sons:

12 And the younger of them said to *his* father, Father, give me the portion of goods that falleth *to me*. And he divided unto them *his* living.

13 And not many days after the younger son gathered all together, and took his journey into a far country, and there wasted his substance with riotous living.

14 And when he had spent all, there arose a mighty famine in that land; and he began to be in want.

15 And he went and joined himself to a citizen of that country; and he sent him into his fields to feed swine.

16 And he would fain have filled his belly with the husks that the swine did eat: and no man gave unto him.

17 And when he came to himself, he said, How many hired servants of my father's have bread enough and to spare, and I perish with hunger!

18 I will arise and go to my father, and will say unto him, Father, I have sinned against heaven, and before thee,

19 And am no more worthy to be called thy son: make me as one of thy hired servants.

20 And he arose, and came to his father. But when he was yet a great way off, his father saw him, and had compassion, and ran, and fell on his neck, and kissed him.

21 And the son said unto him, Father, I have sinned against heaven, and in thy sight, and am no more worthy to be called thy son.

22 But the father said to his servants, Bring forth the best robe, and put *it* on him; and put a ring on his hand, and shoes on *his* feet:

23 And bring hither the fatted calf, and kill *it*; and let us eat, and be merry:

24 For this my son was dead, and is alive again; he was lost, and is found. And they began to be merry.

25 Now his elder son was in the field: and as he came and

drew nigh to the house, he heard musick and dancing.

26 And he called one of the servants, and asked what these things meant.

27 And he said unto him, Thy brother is come; and thy father hath killed the fatted calf, because he hath received him safe and sound.

28 And he was angry, and would not go in: therefore came his father out, and intreated him.

29 And he answering said to *his* father, Lo, these many years do I serve thee, neither transgressed I at any time thy commandment: and yet thou never gavest me a kid, that I might make merry with my friends:

30 But as soon as this thy son was come, which hath devoured thy living with harlots, thou hast killed for him the fatted calf.

31 And he said unto him, Son, thou art ever with me, and all that I have is thine.

32 It was meet that we should make merry, and be glad: for this thy brother was dead, and is alive again; and was lost, and is found.

—LUKE 15:11–32

Left: *The repentant Prodigal Son hopes to be received back into his home as a servant, but his father's joyful welcome will far exceed his expectations.*

THE TWO DEBTORS

41 There was a certain creditor which had two debtors: the one owed five hundred pence, and the other fifty.

42 And when they had nothing to pay, he frankly forgave them both. Tell me therefore, which of them will love him most?

43 Simon answered and said, I suppose that *he*, to whom he forgave most. And he said unto him, Thou hast rightly judged.

—LUKE 7:41–43

THE WISE STEWARD

42 And the Lord said, Who then is that faithful and wise steward, whom *his* lord shall make ruler over his household, to give *them their* portion of meat in due season?

43 Blessed *is* that servant, whom his lord when he cometh shall find so doing.

44 Of a truth I say unto you, that he will make him ruler over all that he hath.

45 But and if that servant say in his heart, My lord delayeth his coming; and shall begin to beat the menservants and maidens, and to eat and drink, and to be drunken;

46 The lord of that servant will come in a day when he looketh not for *him*, and at an hour when he is not aware, and will cut him in sunder, and will appoint him his portion with the unbelievers.

47 And that servant, which knew his lord's will, and prepared not *himself*, neither did according to his will, shall be beaten with many *stripes*.

48 But he that knew not, and did commit things worthy of stripes, shall be beaten with few *stripes*.

—LUKE 12:42–48

ON VOCATION

On Vocation

Previous page: A fifteenth-century portrait of the Madonna and Child, from the school of Verrocchio. Throughout the gospels we see examples of Mary fulfilling her predestined vocation as a mother.

The sound of calling reverberates through the New Testament. Christ calls his disciples from their fishing boats to a new vocation as His witnesses; blind Bartimaeus cries out repeatedly for Christ's help, not to be silenced by the crowd; the disciples call Christ from His sleep during the storm on the lake because they are afraid of drowning. In fact, all of the gospels record an ongoing dialogue between Christ and His fellow men and Christ and God, whom He taught them to call "Our Father."

The theme of vocation runs through many of the parables. In the story of the Wheat and the Tares, country people could identify with the plight of the householder who planted "good seed" in his wheat field only to have an enemy come by night and sow weeds among the wheat. The tares are usually identified as a species of rye grass that tastes bitter and causes dizziness if mixed with wheat flour. These weeds were a common problem in the Middle East, and it was impossible to uproot them while the wheat was growing. The householder told his servants to let the weeds grow up with the wheat until harvest time (when the tares would stand erect, while the wheat bent over from the weight of the grain). Then the weeds could be gathered and burnt and the harvest reaped.

Christ explained this parable to his disciples privately as a story of good and evil in life, which would endure until the end of time. Identifying Himself as "the Son of man" [the householder], He explained that "The field is the world; the good seed are the children of the kingdom; but the tares are the children of the wicked one." Only at the last judgement would the two be separated: "Then shall the righteous shine forth as the sun in the kingdom of their Father."

Mercy, rather than strict justice, is the theme of the Workers in the Vineyard. Here, the employer is God, who finds work for everyone in need and pays each enough to buy food for his family, no matter what time of day he began to work. (The "penny" issued to every vinedresser was a drachma or dinarius—the standard payment for a day's work.) Human notions of justice, as expressed by the workers who started earliest, are likely to reflect selfishness and envy. In this parable, Christ urges self-examination and speaks on behalf of the oppressed. Those who came to work latest (the poor) were treated by the employer with far more kindness than the rich would have shown them—and far more than they had expected.

Faithfulness to one's vocation is emphasized in the parable of the Talents, which is about money (abilities) held in trust. Those servants who took risks by trading with their master's money were commended for increasing it, thus showing responsibility. The servant who took no chances, and handed back the sum originally entrusted to him, was berated for burying his talent in the earth. Although the rabbinical law prescribed this as a means of safekeeping, money becomes productive only in circulation, so this servant's narrow sense of responsibility prevented him from taking full advantage of the opportunities offered by active trade. This message would be underscored by St. Paul in his Epistle to the Romans (12:6): "The gifts we possess differ as they are allotted to us by God's grace, and must be exercised accordingly."

The parable of the Unjust Steward has been a puzzle to interpreters from the beginning. Was Christ really commending the steward who told his master's debtors to falsify their records so they could pay less than they

Below: The underlying lesson of the Talents was to make use of God-given advantages. This message would be reiterated through the teachings of St. Paul.

Above: *In the parable of the Rich Fool, the wealthy man sets too much store by his worldly goods and allows his spiritual life to become impoverished. Here he is seen with such abundant crops that he cannot house them all.*

owed? He had just been fired for mismanagement. By his own admission, he conspired with the debtors to avoid becoming a ditch digger or a beggar. So why did his master praise him as having acted wisely? This parable ends with what has been perceived as an explanation: "for the children of this world are in their generation wiser than the children of light."

Scripture scholar Robert Farrar Capon brings a radically new interpretation to this story in *The Parables of Grace*. In his view, "The unique contribution of this parable to our understanding of Jesus is its insistence that grace cannot come to the world through respectability. Respectability regards only life, success, winning; it will have no truck with the grace that works by death and losing—which is the only kind of grace there is." Pointing out that Christ Himself was considered disreputable by the self-righteous, who conspired to kill Him, he concludes: "This parable…says in story form what Jesus himself said by his life. He was not respectable. He broke the Sabbath. He consorted with crooks. And he died as a criminal. Now at last, in the light of this parable, we see *why* he refused to be respectable: he did it to catch a world that respectability could only terrify and condemn."

There is a strong parallel between the parables of the Lighted Candle and the Body's Lamp (the eye). In the first, Christ's followers are urged to show the light of His mission openly. This had precedent in Hebrew scriptures, where Israel was called the light or lamp of the world. Here, the light is that of Christ Himself.

In the parable of the Body's Lamp, Christ tells his hearers that "when thine eye is single, thy whole body also is full of light." This implies that focusing on Christ and His love—the "one thing necessary" that He commended to Martha, the sister of Lazarus and Mary—will transform one's life.

In the parable of the Rich Fool, Christ warns against the desire for two kinds of wealth: mental and material. First, he tells His disciples to rely entirely upon the Holy Spirit of God when they are threatened by religious or other authorities. They cannot count on well-paid lawyers and well-prepared cases, as others do. Their only security is in their poverty and dependence upon God. Similarly, those who put all their energy into the pursuit of material things are "not rich in God's sight."

Single-mindedness in the cause of discipleship recurs in the twin parables of the Tower Builder and the Warring King. Both challenge Christ's followers to count the cost of their commitment and be ready to persevere despite ridicule, tedium and the very real limitations of their human nature. Self-knowledge and humility are both necessary: one must ask for help in carrying out the required tasks. Paradoxically, only grace can enable one to become fully human, as Christ exemplified humanity in His life and death.

Below: Two latecomers to the vineyard are welcomed by the employer and sent to work. Expecting to receive a lesser wage than the others, they will be surprised to receive a full day's pay—what we would call a living wage.

WHEAT AND TARES

24 Another parable put he forth unto them, saying, The kingdom of heaven is likened unto a man which sowed good seed in his field:

25 But while men slept, his enemy came and sowed tares among the wheat, and went his way.

26 But when the blade was sprung up, and brought forth fruit, then appeared the tares also.

27 So the servants of the householder came and said unto him, Sir, didst not thou sow good seed in thy field? from whence then hath it tares?

28 He said unto them, An enemy hath done this. The servants said unto him, Wilt thou then that we go and gather them up?

29 But he said, Nay; lest while ye gather up the tares, ye root up also the wheat with them.

30 Let both grow together until the harvest: and in the time of harvest I will say to the reapers, Gather ye together first the tares, and bind them in bundles to burn them: but gather the wheat into my barn.

* * *

36 Then Jesus sent the multitude away, and went into the house: and his disciples came unto him, saying, Declare unto us the parable of the tares of the field.

37 He answered and said unto them, He that soweth the good seed is the Son of man;

38 The field is the world; the good seed are the children of the kingdom; but the tares are the children of the wicked *one*;

39 The enemy that sowed them is the devil; the harvest is the end of the world; and the reapers are the angels.

40 As therefore the tares are gathered and burned in the fire; so shall it be in the end of this world.

41 The Son of man shall send forth his angels, and they

shall gather out of his kingdom all things that offend, and them which do iniquity;

42 And shall cast them into a furnace of fire: there shall be wailing and gnashing of teeth.

43 Then shall the righteous shine forth as the sun in the kingdom of their Father. Who hath ears to hear, let him hear.

—MATTHEW 13:24–30, 36–43

Below: One of a series of paintings of stacks of grain by Claude Monet. The theme of a fruitful harvest recurs throughout the Gospels.

WORKERS IN THE VINEYARD

1 For the kingdom of heaven is like unto a man *that is* an householder, which went out early in the morning to hire labourers into his vineyard.

2 And when he had agreed with the labourers for a penny a day, he sent them into his vineyard.

3 And he went out about the third hour, and saw others standing idle in the marketplace,

4 And said unto them; Go ye also into the vineyard, and whatsoever is right I will give you. And they went their way.

5 Again he went out about the sixth and ninth hour, and did likewise.

6 And about the eleventh hour he went out, and found others standing idle, and saith unto them, Why stand ye here all the day idle?

7 They say unto him, Because no man hath hired us. He saith unto them, Go ye also into the vineyard; and whatsoever is right, *that* shall ye receive.

8 So when even was come, the lord of the vineyard saith unto his steward, Call the labourers, and give them *their* hire, beginning from the last unto the first.

9 And when they came that *were hired* about the eleventh hour, they received every man a penny.

Right: *Vincent Van Gogh's colorful painting of workers toiling in a vineyard, 1888.*

10 But when the first came, they supposed that they should have received more; and they likewise received every man a penny.

11 And when they had received *it*, they murmured against the goodman of the house,

12 Saying, These last have wrought *but* one hour, and thou hast made them equal unto us, which have borne the burden and heat of the day.

13 But he answered one of them, and said, Friend, I do thee no wrong: didst not thou agree with me for a penny?

14 Take *that thine is*, and go thy way: I will give unto this last, even as unto thee.

15 Is it not lawful for me to do what I will with mine own? Is thine eye evil, because I am good?

16 So the last shall be first, and the first last: for many be called, but few chosen.

—MATTHEW 20:1–16

THE TALENTS

14 For *the kingdom of heaven is* as a man travelling into a far country, *who* called his own servants, and delivered unto them his goods.

15 And unto one he gave five talents, to another two, and to another one; to every man according to his several ability; and straightway took his journey.

16 Then he that had received the five talents went and traded with the same, and made *them* other five talents.

17 And likewise he that *had received* two, he also gained other two.

18 But he that had received one went and digged in the earth, and hid his lord's money.

19 After a long time the lord of those servants cometh, and reckoneth with them.

20 And so he that had received five talents came and brought other five talents, saying, Lord, thou deliveredst unto me five talents: behold, I have gained beside them five talents more.

21 His lord said unto him, Well done, *thou* good and faithful servant: thou hast been faithful over a few things, I will make thee ruler over many things: enter thou into the joy of thy lord.

22 He also that had received two talents came and said, Lord, thou deliveredst unto me two talents: behold, I have gained two other talents beside them.

23 His lord said unto him, Well done, good and faithful servant; thou hast been faithful over a few things, I will make thee ruler over many things: enter thou into the joy of thy lord.

24 Then he which had received the one talent came and said, Lord, I knew thee that thou art an hard man, reaping where thou hast not sown, and gathering where thou hast not strawed:

25 And I was afraid, and went and hid thy talent in the earth: lo, *there* thou hast *that is* thine.

26 His lord answered and said unto him, *Thou* wicked and slothful servant, thou knewest that I reap where I sowed not, and gather where I have not strawed:

27 Thou oughtest therefore to have put my money to the exchangers, and *then* at my coming I should have received mine own with usury.

28 Take therefore the talent from him, and give *it* unto him which hath ten talents.

29 For unto every one that hath shall be given, and he shall have abundance: but from him that hath not shall be taken away even that which he hath.

30 And cast ye the unprofitable servant into outer darkness: there shall be weeping and gnashing of teeth.

—MATTHEW 25:14–30

THE UNJUST STEWARD

1 And he said also unto his disciples, There was a certain rich man, which had a steward; and the same was accused unto him that he had wasted his goods.

2 And he called him, and said unto him, How is it that I hear this of thee? give an account of thy stewardship; for thou mayest be no longer steward.

3 Then the steward said within himself, What shall I do? for my lord taketh away from me the stewardship: I cannot dig; to beg I am ashamed.

4 I am resolved what to do, that, when I am put out of the stewardship, they may receive me into their houses.

5 So he called every one of his lord's debtors *unto him*, and said unto the first, How much owest thou unto my lord?

6 And he said, An hundred measures of oil. And he said unto him, Take thy bill, and sit down quickly, and write fifty.

7 Then said he to another, And how much owest thou? And he said, An hundred measures of wheat. And he said unto him, Take thy bill, and write fourscore.

8 And the lord commended the unjust steward, because he had done wisely: for the children of this world are in their generation wiser than the children of light.

9 And I say unto you, Make to yourselves friends of the mammon of unrighteousness; that, when ye fail, they may receive you into everlasting habitations.

10 He that is faithful in that which is least is faithful also in much: and he that is unjust in the least is unjust also in much.

11 If therefore ye have not been faithful in the unrighteous mammon, who will commit to your trust the true *riches*?

Below: Commentators have attached many different interpretations to the meaning of the parable of the Unjust Steward.

Opposite: Having suffered a crisis of faith, St. Augustine of Hippo (depicted here by Botticelli) dedicated himself to his vocation and went on to become one of the most influential scholars in history. The parable of the Body's Lamp advocates a single-minded focus on Christ's teachings.

12 And if ye have not been faithful in that which is another man's, who shall give you that which is your own?

13 No servant can serve two masters: for either he will hate the one, and love the other; or else he will hold to the one, and despise the other. Ye cannot serve God and mammon.

—LUKE 16:1–13

THE LIGHTED CANDLE

21 And he said unto them, Is a candle brought to be put under a bushel, or under a bed? and not to be set on a candlestick?

22 For there is nothing hid, which shall not be manifested; neither was any thing kept secret, but that it should come abroad.

23 If any man have ears to hear, let him hear.

—MARK 4:21–23

THE BODY'S LAMP

33 No man, when he hath lighted a candle, putteth *it* in a secret place, neither under a bushel, but on a candlestick, that they which come in may see the light.

34 The light of the body is the eye: therefore when thine eye is single, thy whole body also is full of light; but when *thine eye* is evil, thy body also *is* full of darkness.

35 Take heed therefore that the light which is in thee be not darkness.

36 If thy whole body therefore *be* full of light, having no part dark, the whole shall be full of light, as when the bright shining of a candle doth give thee light.

—LUKE 11:33–36

THE RICH FOOL

Opposite: Jesus taught that it is more important to concentrate on our inner lives than on material possessions. By multiplying the loaves and the fishes, He demonstrated that God will provide for our needs.

Below: The Rich Fool counting his money and congratulating himself only hours before his unexpected death.

16 And he spake a parable unto them, saying, The ground of a certain rich man brought forth plentifully:

17 And he thought within himself, saying, What shall I do, because I have no room where to bestow my fruits?

18 And he said, This will I do: I will pull down my barns, and build greater; and there will I bestow all my fruits and my goods.

19 And I will say to my soul, Soul, thou hast much goods laid up for many years; take thine ease, eat, drink, *and* be merry.

20 But God said unto him, *Thou* fool, this night thy soul shall be required of thee: then whose shall those things be, which thou hast provided?

21 So *is* he that layeth up treasure for himself, and is not rich toward God.

—LUKE 12:16–21

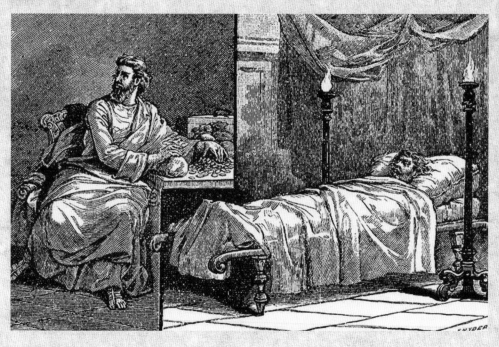

THE TOWER BUILDER AND THE WARRING KING

28 For which of you, intending to build a tower, sitteth not down first, and counteth the cost, whether he have *sufficient* to finish it?

29 Lest haply, after he hath laid the foundation, and is not able to finish *it*, all that behold *it* begin to mock him,

30 Saying, This man began to build, and was not able to finish.

31 Or what king, going to make war against another king, sitteth not down first, and consulteth whether he be able with ten thousand to meet him that cometh against him with twenty thousand?

32 Or else, while the other is yet a great way off, he sendeth an ambassage, and desireth conditions of peace.

—LUKE 14:28–32

Right: Gustave Doré's nineteenth-century engraving of Christ in the temple with elders.

On
Spirituality

ON SPIRITUALITY

The generosity of God as compared to man overflows in all the parables on spirituality, which encompasses both prayer and grace. In the parable of the Watchful Servants, which is usually interpreted as a warning, the deeper meaning is one of reassurance. Not only are the Watchful Servants commended for staying on the alert for their lord's coming, when he *does* come, he turns the tables by serving them. This recalls the Last Supper, when Christ astonished and humbled his apostles by putting a towel around his waist like a servant and washing their feet in the customary purification ritual. When Peter protested, saying, "Thou shalt never wash my feet," Christ told him: "If I wash thee not, thou hast no part with me" (John 13:8). Then Peter assented wholeheartedly, putting aside the conventional notions of the Master/disciple relationship for the new model of a mutual love beyond human comprehension.

The parable of the Great Supper is another illustration of unexpected graciousness. Christ's party-giver, God, is eager to fill his house with guests. First, He invites all the "right" people, but they send their regrets for all the right reasons: business to attend to and so forth. The would-be host is affronted and sends all

Below: *Goya's portrait of St. Peter in fervent prayer with his emblem, the keys to the Kingdom of Heaven.*

over town for the local "untouchables"—the blind, the maimed and others whom no respectable householder would think of inviting. Having filled the house with these unlikely guests—whom those on the original guest list wouldn't be caught dead with—the host is entirely content. His total commitment to graciousness is satisfied by giving to those who are shunned by the worldly-wise. He goes so far as to say that "none of those men which were bidden shall taste of my supper." This forecasts the saying found in the parable of the lost sheep: "Joy shall be in heaven over one sinner that repenteth, more than over ninety and nine just persons, which need no repentance."

Another simile on the unseen working of grace is that of the Seed Growing Secretly. The farmer scatters his seed in the field and goes about his business as the crop springs up and flourishes "he knoweth not how." His part is a small one—the real work is done by grace, which will create new life where the smallest sign of willingness is discerned. It operates independently of human notions of justice, self-righteousness, or what must and must not be done to please God. One has already pleased God by the mere fact of being human. It is the act of being itself that gives one an unlimited claim upon the goodness of God as Creator, Redeemer and Sanctifier of all that is.

God's predilection for the least and the lost is emphasized again in Christ's reply to the indignant Pharisees, who demanded: "Why do the disciples of John and of the Pharisees fast, but thy disciples fast not?" As usual, they were seeking to put Him in the wrong because of envy. He had called Levi, one of the despised tax collectors, to follow Him, and ended up dining at Levi's house, which scandalized the self-righteous. Their idea of spirituality was a kind of moral bookkeeping, whereby one fulfilled all the outward prescriptions of the Law. Christ's radical view was that those in most need of grace were the ones for whom He was "the bridegroom." And while He was present among them, they could not fast and had no need to do so. This is another

Page 55: The Virgin Mary, an exemplar of great spirituality, is honored by the Risen Christ in this moving Renaissance work by Titian.

variation on the theme of the Great Supper, which turned the prevailing notion of grace on its head and made winners of the world's losers.

The parable of the Budding Fig Tree focuses again on the theme of unbounded grace and the goodness to be poured out upon the world through Christ's death and resurrection. The summer foretold by the leafing out of the fig tree "and all the trees" is the unending summer ushered in by the coming of the kingdom of God. It would be manifested fully at the end of time, and Christ's presence in the world was the living sign of that fulfillment: He told His disciples that "Heaven and earth shall pass away: but my words shall not pass away." As the visible, audible Word of God in the world, Christ alone could draw all things to Himself and reconcile them to God.

The Pharisees were offended again when Christ taught that it was not the things a person ate and drank that could defile him, but the things that came out of his mouth at the prompting of an evil heart. As an example, He cited: "murders, adulteries, fornications, thefts, false witness, blasphemies." This ran counter to the whole idea of outward observance as a protection against inner corruption. The contrast was emphasized in the conclusion: "These are the things which defile a man: but to eat with unwashen hands defileth not a man."

Christ's words on inward purity were reinforced by His condemnation of the Pharisees as the blind leading the blind, with the result that "both shall fall into a ditch." This was one of the many occasions on which Christ taught that true spirituality looked always to the free gift of grace, rather than to self-serving ideas of how to compel God's approbation. The Pharisees of this world were censured for multiplying the burdens of religion until they became heavier than people could bear, thus making them feel cut off from God rather than at peace with Him.

One of the best-loved parables is that of the Birds of Heaven and the Lilies of the Field—radical examples of the

spirituality of being. The disciples are encouraged to surrender their everyday concerns about food, clothing and other necessities of life and trust in God to provide for them as they seek first the Kingdom. Examples are drawn from nature, showing how the birds are fed and the lilies clothed in brilliant colors without any forethought on their part. The disciples were empowered by grace to take this message fully to heart only after they received the Holy Spirit in the wake of Christ's ascension into heaven. Not until the Acts of the Apostles do we see them consistently following Christ's example and encouragement to "Sell that ye have and give alms; provide yourselves bags which wax not old, a treasure in the heavens that faileth not, where no thief approaches nor moth corrupteth." This parable ends with the telling words that have inspired generations of people in search of true spirituality: "For where your treasure is, there will your heart be also."

THE GREAT SUPPER

16 Then said he unto him, A certain man made a great supper, and bade many:

17 And sent his servant at supper time to say to them that were bidden, Come; for all things are now ready.

18 And they all with one *consent* began to make excuse. The first said unto him, I have bought a piece of ground, and I must needs go and see it: I pray thee have me excused.

19 And another said, I have bought five yoke of oxen, and I go to prove them: I pray thee have me excused.

20 And another said, I have married a wife, and therefore I cannot come.

21 So that servant came, and shewed his lord these things. Then the master of the house being angry said to his servant, Go out quickly into the streets and lanes of the city, and bring in hither the poor, and the maimed, and the halt, and the blind.

22 And the servant said, Lord, it is done as thou hast commanded, and yet there is room.

23 And the lord said unto the servant, Go out into the highways and hedges, and compel *them* to come in, that my house may be filled.

24 For I say unto you, That none of those men which were bidden shall taste of my supper.

—LUKE 14:16–24

THE WATCHFUL SERVANTS

35 Let your loins be girded about, and *your* lights burning;

36 And ye yourselves like unto men that wait for their lord, when he will return from the wedding; that when he cometh and knocketh, they may open unto him immediately.

37 Blessed *are* those servants, whom the lord when he cometh shall find watching: verily I say unto you, that he shall gird himself, and make them to sit down to meat, and will come forth and serve them.

38 And if he shall come in the second watch, or come in the third watch, and find *them* so, blessed are those servants.

39 And this know, that if the goodman of the house had known what hour the thief would come, he would have watched, and not have suffered his house to be broken through.

40 Be ye therefore ready also: for the Son of man cometh at an hour when ye think not.

Below: Two of Christ's watchful servants are surprised and overjoyed when He reveals Himself to them at Emmaus after His resurrection. The luminous painting (1629) is by Velazquez.

—LUKE 12:35–40

THE SEED GROWING SECRETLY

26 And he said, So is the kingdom of God, as if a man should cast seed into the ground;

27 And should sleep, and rise night and day, and the seed should spring and grow up, he knoweth not how.

28 For the earth bringeth forth fruit of herself; first the blade, then the ear, after that the full corn in the ear.

29 But when the fruit is brought forth, immediately he putteth in the sickle, because the harvest is come.

—MARK 4:26–29

THE BUDDING FIG TREE

29 And he spake to them a parable; Behold the fig tree, and all the trees;

30 When they now shoot forth, ye see and know of your own selves that summer is now nigh at hand.

31 So likewise ye, when ye see these things come to pass, know ye that the kingdom of God is nigh at hand.

32 Verily I say unto you, This generation shall not pass away, till all be fulfilled.

33 Heaven and earth shall pass away: but my words shall not pass away.

—LUKE 21:29–33

PRAYER AND FASTING

14 And as he passed by, he saw Levi the *son* of Alphaeus sitting at the receipt of custom, and said unto him, Follow me. And he arose and followed him.

15 And it came to pass, that, as Jesus sat at meat in his house, many publicans and sinners sat also together with Jesus and his disciples: for there were many, and they followed him.

16 And when the scribes and Pharisees saw him eat with publicans and sinners, they said unto his disciples, How is it that he eateth and drinketh with publicans and sinners?

17 When Jesus heard *it*, he saith unto them, They that are whole have no need of the physician, but they that are sick: I came not to call the righteous, but sinners to repentance.

18 And the disciples of John and of the Pharisees used to fast: and they come and say unto him, Why do the disciples of John and of the Pharisees fast, but thy disciples fast not?

19 And Jesus said unto them, Can the children of the bridechamber fast, while the bridegroom is with them? as long as they have the bridegroom with them, they cannot fast.

20 But the days will come, when the bridegroom shall be taken away from them, and then shall they fast in those days.

—MARK 2:14–20

Below: Titian's St. John the Evangelist, who followed Christ's example of prayer, fasting and almsgiving throughout his long lifetime. He was the only apostle who did not die a martyr's death.

THE BIRDS OF HEAVEN AND THE LILIES OF THE FIELD

Opposite: A detail of Van Gogh's painting of irises. The parable of the Lilies of the Field teaches that we should not worry about material concerns like clothing, since nature's most beautiful flowers are endowed with their outer appearance purely by God's care, rather than by their own efforts.

22 And he said unto his disciples, Therefore I say unto you, Take no thought for your life, what ye shall eat; neither for the body, what ye shall put on.

23 The life is more than meat, and the body *is more* than raiment.

24 Consider the ravens: for they neither sow nor reap; which neither have storehouse nor barn; and God feedeth them: how much more are ye better than the fowls?

25 And which of you with taking thought can add to his stature one cubit?

26 If ye then be not able to do that thing which is least, why take ye thought for the rest?

27 Consider the lilies how they grow: they toil not, they spin not; and yet I say unto you, that Solomon in all his glory was not arrayed like one of these.

28 If then God so clothe the grass, which is to day in the field, and to morrow is cast into the oven; how much more *will he clothe you*, O ye of little faith?

29 And seek not ye what ye shall eat, or what ye shall drink, neither be ye of doubtful mind.

30 For all these things do the nations of the world seek after: and your Father knoweth that ye have need of these things.

31 But rather seek ye the kingdom of God; and all these things shall be added unto you.

—LUKE 12:22–31

ON INWARD PURITY

Below: *Christ is baptized by his cousin John, "the voice of one crying in the wilderness," in this depiction by Giotto. The rite signified inward purity and revealed Christ as the promised Messiah.*

10 And he called the multitude, and said unto them, Hear, and understand:

11 Not that which goeth into the mouth defileth a man; but that which cometh out of the mouth, this defileth a man.

12 Then came his disciples, and said unto him, Knowest thou that the Pharisees were offended, after they heard this saying?

13 But he answered and said, Every plant, which my heavenly Father hath not planted, shall be rooted up.

14 Let them alone: they be blind leaders of the blind. And if the blind lead the blind, both shall fall into the ditch.

15 Then answered Peter and said unto him, Declare unto us this parable.

16 And Jesus said, Are ye also yet without understanding?

17 Do not ye yet understand, that whatsoever entereth in at the mouth goeth into the belly, and is cast out into the draught?

18 But those things which proceed out of the mouth come forth from the heart; and they defile the man.

19 For out of the heart proceed evil thoughts, murders, adulteries, fornications, thefts, false witness, blasphemies:

20 These are the *things* which defile a man: but to eat with unwashen hands defileth not a man.

—MATTHEW 15:10–20

On Doorways
Open and Shut

On Doorways
Open and Shut

Previous page:
Goya's painting of
the crucified Christ,
whose death reopened
the doors of eternal life
to humankind.

The old order and the new are contrasted in a number of parables that speak of doorways, gates and guardians of these openings. In the parable of the Divided Realm, Christ confounded those critics who accused Him of doing good works through sorcery rather than by the power of God. He pointed out that the kingdom of Satan (the Adversary) was inherently divided against itself and would ultimately fail. It was powerless against the Kingdom of God, which worked toward healing and happiness, not self-destruction. This statement was reinforced by the story of the Strong Man Bound—another type of the evil powers that Christ had come to overthrow and dispossess. Identifying Himself with the Suffering Servant prophesied by Isaiah, He proclaimed Himself the victor who would overcome the strong and redistribute their goods ("spoils") to the needy. The Jews were awaiting the time predicted in the words of the Assumption of Moses: "His Kingdom shall appear throughout all His creation; And Satan shall be no more; And sorrow shall depart with him." In these parables, Christ announced the arrival of the promised Kingdom through His power to overcome all evil.

Luke placed the parable of the Defendant with a series of warnings about the coming crisis of choice between old and new. These warnings are just as applicable today, in the face of world hunger, overpopulation and a growing schism between the rich and the rest of us. Reflective people of many faiths see the potential for widespread breakdowns of the social order under these stresses. However, the solution does not lie in violence, but in seeking reconciliation before estrangement becomes total. The counsel to agree with one's adversary on the way to the magistrate has wide-ranging implications. Willingness to keep open the door to mutual understanding, whether between persons or nations, builds peace rather than conflict.

The parable of the Closed Door (also called the Narrow Gate) is often interpreted as a warning, but it is, in fact, an invitation to accept grace, the unexpected gift beyond our hopes. Christ is the "master of the house" who "is risen up" to admit everyone who has embraced His example of unconditional love. Those who knock at the door demanding entrance but are left standing outside are like the guest who came to the Wedding Feast without the right clothing. They have not fully understood that they must put off the old grasping, selfish ways and put on what St. Paul called "the armour of light"—willingness to follow Christ's example of selfless love and trust in God. In this parable, Christ emphasizes again that the kingdom will be filled from the four corners of the earth and that "there be last which shall be first and there are first which shall be last."

Below: St. John the Baptist, painted by Andrea del Verrocchio, performed his baptisms to open the door of faith to those who would be cleansed of their sins.

In the parable of the Doorkeeper, watchfulness is the quality that admits "the master" and wins his approbation. Grace may come at any time: "at even [evening], or at midnight, or at the cock-crowing, or in the morning." The doorkeeper who is vigilant will not lose any opportunity to admit life-giving grace, whereas the one who is sleeping misses the chance to experience spiritual growth through openness to new ideas, new courage and the "daily bread" of God's compassionate support.

"How much more" is the theme of the Son's Request, which compares God to a conscientious human father who answers a child's request for food. Christ shocks his listeners into awareness when He asks: "What man is there of you, whom if his son ask bread, will give him a stone? Or if he ask a fish, will he give him a serpent?" He points out that the goodness of God is far beyond that of human beings, no matter how well-intentioned, and that perseverance in prayer will always be rewarded in God's own time: "For every one that asketh receiveth; and he that seeketh findeth; and to him that knocketh it shall be opened."

In ancient Middle Eastern weddings, the bridegroom was the focus of attention rather than the bride. In the parable of the Wise and Foolish Virgins, Christ is the bridegroom. All the bride's friends gather by night to await his arrival and attend him to the ceremony, but he is delayed and half the girls fall asleep and let their lamps go out. They beg the others for oil to rekindle their lamps, but are refused and hurry off to find a store that may still be open. Meanwhile, the whole bridal party enters the festive house and shuts the door. Failure to pay attention to what they were doing caused them to miss their opportunity, like the drowsy porter who fell asleep while awaiting his master's return from a journey. The interpretation of this parable as one of the Parousia, or Second Coming, did not arise until the first century AD, when the early Christian Church began to describe itself as the Bride of Christ.

The much-loved parable of the Good Shepherd was told shortly before Christ's passion and death. It sums up his ministry in the moving image of the shepherd who lays down his life for his sheep. When Christ described Himself as "the door of the sheep," His meaning was clear to the country people of Palestine. It was customary for the shepherd to gather his flock every evening and to pen them up in a rude enclosure. He slept at the entrance, guarding the flock with his own body. The sheep would not step over his sleeping form any more than they would answer the call of another shepherd ("the hireling"). If a wolf or other predator tried to get in, the shepherd would defend the flock with his life, while the hireling fled. In this parable, Christ referred to false prophets and other imposters as thieves and robbers, "but the sheep did not hear them…for they know not the voice of strangers."

This parable is so important that it is repeated immediately and expanded upon in the words: "I am the good shepherd: the good shepherd giveth his life for the sheep. [I] know my sheep, and am known of mine." The universality of Christ's mission is seen in the concluding verse: "Other sheep I have, which are not of this fold: them also I must bring, and they shall hear my voice; and there shall be one fold, and one shepherd." The theme of ultimate unity and peace is the consoling note struck by this parable as Christ "set his face toward Jerusalem" to lay down His life and take it up again.

Below: Christ presides over the Last Supper in a Renaissance painting by Titian, which captures the intimacy and homeliness of His relationship with His followers.

THE DIVIDED REALM AND THE STRONG MAN BOUND

Opposite: Botticelli's painting portrays the virtue of fortitude. Jesus taught in these parables that moral strength is more important than physical might.

17 But he, knowing their thoughts, said unto them, Every kingdom divided against itself is brought to desolation; and a house *divided* against a house falleth.

18 If Satan also be divided against himself, how shall his kingdom stand? because ye say that I cast out devils through Beelzebub.

19 And if I by Beelzebub cast out devils, by whom do your sons cast *them* out? therefore shall they be your judges.

20 But if I with the finger of God cast out devils, no doubt the kingdom of God is come upon you.

21 When a strong man armed keepeth his palace, his goods are in peace:

22 But when a stronger than he shall come upon him, and overcome him, he taketh from him all his armour wherein he trusted, and divideth his spoils.

—LUKE 11:17–22

THE DEFENDANT

58 When thou goest with thine adversary to the magistrate, *as thou art* in the way, give diligence that thou mayest be delivered from him; lest he hale thee to the judge, and the judge deliver thee to the officer, and the officer cast thee into prison.

59 I tell thee, thou shalt not depart thence, till thou hast paid the very last mite.

—LUKE 12:58–59

THE CLOSED DOOR

Opposite and below:
*Christ's death on the
cross (Roger van der
Weyden, below) and
subsequent ascension
(Raphael, opposite)
represent doors closing
on His mortal life and
then reopening as He
enters the Kingdom
of Heaven.*

24 Strive to enter in at the strait gate: for many, I say unto you, will seek to enter in, and shall not be able.

25 When once the master of the house is risen up, and hath shut to the door, and ye begin to stand wihout, and to knock at the door, saying, Lord, Lord, open unto us; and he shall answer and say unto you, I know you not whence ye are:

26 Then shall ye begin to say, We have eaten and drunk in thy presence, and thou hast taught in our streets.

27 But he shall say, I tell you, I know not when ye are; depart from me, all ye workers of iniquity.

28 There shall be weeping and gnashing of teeth, when ye shall see Abraham, and Isaac, and Jacob, and all the prophets, in the kingdom of God, and you *yourselves* thrust out.

29 And they shall come from the east, and *from* the west, and from the north, and *from* the south, and shall sit down in the kingdom of God.

30 And, behold, there are last which shall be first, and there are first which shall be last.

—LUKE 13:24–30

THE SON'S REQUEST

Below: Renoir's painting of his child at play (1905) recalls the theme of parental love addressed in the parable of the Son's Request.

9   Or what man is there of you, whom if his son ask bread, will he give him a stone?

10 Or if he ask a fish, will he give him a serpent?

11 If ye then, being evil, know how to give good gifts unto your children, how much more shall your Father which is in heaven give good things to them that ask him?

12 Therefore all things whatsoever ye would that men should do to you, do ye even so to them: for this is the law and the prophets.

—MATTHEW 7:9–12

THE WISE AND FOOLISH VIRGINS

1   Then shall the kingdom of heaven be likened unto ten virgins, which took their lamps, and went forth to meet the bridegroom.

2   And five of them were wise, and five *were* foolish.

3   They that were foolish took their lamps, and took no oil with them:

4   But the wise took oil in their vessels with their lamps.

5   While the bridegroom tarried, they all slumbered and slept.

6   And at midnight there was a cry made, Behold, the bridegroom cometh; go ye out to meet him.

7   Then all those virgins arose, and trimmed their lamps.

8   And the foolish said unto the wise, Give us of your oil; for our lamps are gone out.

9   But the wise answered, saying, *Not so*; lest there be not enough for us and you: but go ye rather to them that sell, and buy for yourselves.

10 And while they went to buy, the bridegroom came; and they that were ready went in with him to the marriage: and the door was shut.

11 Afterward came also the other virgins, saying, Lord, Lord, open to us.

12 But he answered and said, Verily I say unto you, I know you not.

13 Watch therefore, for ye know neither the day nor the hour wherein the Son of man cometh.

Above: A nineteenth-century illustration of the Wise and Foolish Virgins awaiting the coming of the bridegroom: those who fell asleep and let their lamps go out were barred from the wedding feast.

—MATTHEW 25:1–13

THE GOOD SHEPHERD

Opposite: Many of the parables and other stories of Christ's life and teachings concern the protection of innocent animals, who represent God's "flock," or children. St. Francis of Assissi, the patron saint of animals, features in this painting by Giotto.

1 Verily, verily, I say unto you, He that entereth not by the door into the sheepfold, but climbeth up some other way, the same is a thief and a robber.

2 But he that entereth in by the door is the shepherd of the sheep.

3 To him the porter openeth; and the sheep hear his voice: and he calleth his own sheep by name, and leadeth them out.

4 And when he putteth forth his own sheep, he goeth before them, and the sheep follow him: for they know his voice.

5 And a stranger will they not follow, but will flee from him: for they know not the voice of strangers.

6 This parable spake Jesus unto them: but they understood not what things they were which he spake unto them.

7 Then said Jesus unto them again, Verily, verily, I say unto you, I am the door of the sheep.

8 All that ever came before me are thieves and robbers: but the sheep did not hear them.

9 I am the door: by me if any man enter in, he shall be saved, and shall go in and out, and find pasture.

10 The thief cometh not, but for to steal, and to kill, and to destroy: I am come that they might have life, and that they might have *it* more abundantly.

* * *

13 The hireling fleeth, because he is an hireling, and careth not for the sheep.

14 I am the good shepherd, and know my *sheep*, and am known of mine.

15 As the Father knoweth me, even so know I the Father: and I lay down my life for the sheep.

16 And other sheep I have, which are not of this fold: them also I must bring, and they shall hear my voice; and there shall be one fold, *and* one shepherd.

—JOHN 10:1–16

INDEX OF PARABLES

Page numbers in *italics* refer to illustrations.

The Glory of the NATIVITY

The Glory of the NATIVITY

CLARE HAWORTH-MADEN
Editor

Saraband

Page 1: Madonna and Child with Saints John the Baptist and Sebastian, *by Pietro Perugino, 1493.*

Page 2: *A detail from* The Adoration of the Magi, *by Fra Angelico with Filippo Lippi, c. 1452–3.*

Page 3: *A detail from Giotto's* The Flight Into Egypt, *c. 1304–6.*

Published by Saraband (Scotland) Limited,
The Arthouse, 752–756 Argyle Street,
Glasgow G3 8UJ, Scotland
hermes@saraband.net

Copyright © 2004 Saraband (Scotland) Ltd.

ISBN: 1-887354-37-9

Printed in China

10 9 8 7 6 5 4 3 2

Acknowledgements

Extracts from the Authorized Version of the Bible (The King James Bible), the rights in which are vested in the Crown, are reproduced by permission of the Crown's Patentee, Cambridge University Press.

The publisher would like to thank the following people for their assistance in the preparation of this book: Clare Haworth-Maden, Debbie Hayes, Sara Hunt, Phoebe Wong, Nicola Gillies, and Wendy J. Ciaccia Eurell. Grateful acknowledgement is also made for the illustrations featured in this book, which are reproduced by courtesy of Planet Art, 2002 Arttoday.com, Inc., and CorelDraw, except that of page 20, which is courtesy of Saraband Image Library.

This book is fondly dedicated to Robin Sommer.

Contents

Introduction

For unto us a child is born, unto us a son is given: and the governments shall be upon his shoulder: and his name shall be called Wonderful, Counsellor, The mighty God, The everlasting Father, The Prince of Peace.

Of the increase of his government and peace there shall be no end, upon the throne of David, and upon his kingdom, to order it, and to establish it with judgment and with justice from henceforth even for ever. The zeal of the LORD of hosts will perform this.

—ISAIAH 9:6–7

Right: Titian's Madonna and Child *is a touching evocation of the Virgin Mary's awe at finding herself the mother of the son of God, as well as of her tenderness for the divine infant.*

Every year on December 25, Christians celebrate the birth, or Nativity, of Jesus Christ, which occurred over two thousand years ago. No other birth has been depicted so frequently by artists over the centuries as that of the Christ child, while the carols that the Christian community sings during Advent, and the Nativity plays performed by children, have made even nonpracticing Christians familiar with the events surrounding Christ's birth.

Our knowledge of the Nativity stems from the New Testament gospels of St. Matthew and St. Luke, parts of which are reproduced in the pages that follow. Yet as we will see, underlying their accounts is a far more complex, and ancient, story than a straightforward reading of their words suggests.

The Gospels of St. Matthew and St. Luke

Of the four gospels of the New Testament, only those of St. Matthew and St. Luke tell of Christ's birth and the circumstances surrounding it. Scholars have suggested that Mark, who is believed to have been John Mark, an associate of Barnabas, Paul, and Peter, the first pope, was more concerned with cutting to the chase and describing the actions and work of Jesus, the man, in an attempt to draw Roman Gentiles to Christianity, while the intention of John, one of Christ's apostles, in writing his gospel was similarly to expand upon Jesus' teaching and message and thus to deepen the faith of existing believers.

Although the ultimate aim of Matthew and Luke's gospels was certainly also to inform, convince, and convert nonbelievers, as well as to strengthen the devotion of Christians, it seems that their purpose, as well as the audiences that they targeted, differed subtly from those of Mark and John.

Matthew is thought to have been Matthew Levi, another of Christ's apostles, who was primarily writing for fellow Jews, whether or not they had become Christians. Luke, on the other hand, is believed to have been a Syrian physician from Antioch—and thus a Gentile Christian—whose gospel was addressed to Theophilus, a Greek, "That thou mightest know the certainty of those things, wherein thou hast been instructed" (Luke 1:4), suggesting that Theophilus was either interested in becoming a Christian or a recent convert. It therefore seems that Luke's gospel was primarily aimed at a Gentile readership, and that Luke was furthermore concerned with presenting a factual story of Jesus' life as related by those "which from the beginning were eyewitnesses, and ministers of the word" (Luke 1:2), one of whom may have been the Virgin Mary herself.

Jesus, the Messiah

Reflecting the different preoccupations of Matthew and Luke's Jewish and Gentile readerships, the theme running through Matthew's gospel is that Jesus is the Jewish Messiah whose coming was prophesied in the Old Testament, while that of Luke is that Jesus is the savior of humankind, and not just of the "children of Israel," God's "chosen people."

Although both include Christ's line of descent in their gospels (Matthew 1:1–17 and Luke 3:23–38), and King David is common to both, the lists of Jesus' forebears not only differ, but while Matthew traces his ancestors back to Abraham (the father of the Hebrew people), Luke goes farther, to God, the creator of Adam, the first man, thereby emphasizing that Jesus was truly the "son of God" (and, indeed, Jesus often addresses God as "Father" in the gospels).

That Jesus counted King David, the founder of the royal Judean dynasty, among His ancestors has profound importance for Jews, who regard much of the period when David ruled over a united Israel as a golden age. On his death (which, historians speculate, occurred between 1018 and 970 BC), David proclaimed that God is "the tower of salvation for his king: and sheweth mercy to his anointed,

unto David, and to his seed for evermore" (2 Samuel 51). "Messiah," which is derived from the Hebrew *mashiah*, means "anointed one," as does "Christ," the anglicized version of the Greek *Christos*, the significance of being anointed lying in the Jewish practice of dedicating a person or object to a sacred purpose through anointment with oil, symbolizing the Holy Spirit.

At the time of Christ's Nativity, the once mighty nation of Israel was in ruins. Palestine, and thus Judea, was now part of Syria, a dominion of the Roman Emperor Augustus

Right: *The Old Testament prophet Jeremiah (depicted here by Michelangelo), who prophesied Christ's Nativity, ended his days in Egypt following the destruction of Jerusalem in 585 BC by the forces of the Babylonian King Nebuchadnezzar.*

Caesar (Octavian) that was governed by the pro-Roman Edomite King Herod the Great. This humiliating state of affairs intensified the Jewish people's longing for the coming of their Messiah, who, the Old Testament prophets had promised, would destroy Israel's enemies, restore the nation of Israel, and recreate the kingdom of God on Earth under his righteous, and peaceful, rule. They expected the Messiah to be a descendant of David, as foretold, for instance, by Jeremiah: "Behold, the days come, saith the LORD, that I will raise unto David a righteous Branch, and a King shall reign and prosper, and shall execute judgment and justice in the earth. In his days Judah shall be saved,

and Israel shall dwell safely: and this is his name whereby he shall be called THE LORD OUR RIGHTEOUSNESS" (Jeremiah 23:5–6). And in Matthew 21:9, we are told that on Jesus' entry into Jerusalem, He was hailed as the "Son of David," thereby underlining the link between Jesus, David, and the Messiah. Matthew seems to further emphasize Jesus' status as the Davidic Messiah by specifying (in Matthew 1:17) that three sets of fourteen generations preceded Christ's birth, for in the Hebrew system of numerology, the Hebrew characters that make up David's name add up to fourteen. In addition, the eras covered by those generations represent the respective pre-eminence of the prophets, kings, and priests, the implication being that Jesus' birth had initiated a new generation, and consequently a new age.

It may seem strange that both Matthew and Luke state that Jesus was descended from David through Joseph, who, after all, was not actually His father. The explanation may be that they were asserting His legal right, as a child whose mother was married to Joseph, to claim David as His ancestor.

Above: Solomon was the last king to rule over a united Israel. The son of King David and Bathsheba, "her that had been the wife of Urias [Uriah]" (Matthew 1:6), was renowned for his wisdom, his judgment in deciding which of two women fighting over a child was its mother being particularly celebrated.

Time and time again the gospels draw a parallel between the events of Jesus' life and the Messiah described by the Old Testament prophets (see, for example, Isaiah 53 and Psalm 22, "a psalm of David"), a connection that Matthew frequently stresses with the words: "Now all this was done, that it might be fulfilled which was spoken of the Lord by the prophet" (Matthew 1:22). The name "Jesus," which, as a variant of Joshua, means "God saves" in Hebrew, is redolent of the Messiah, too, and Matthew tells us that an angel instructed Joseph to call Mary's unborn child "Jesus: for he shall save his people from their sins." Jesus asserted His status and mission in Luke 21:8 ("I am *Christ*") and Luke 24:46, when, after His resurrection, He confirmed to His disciples that He was indeed the Messiah of whose coming the prophets had told: "These *are* the words which I spake unto you, while I was yet with you, that all things must be fulfilled, which were written in the law of Moses, and *in* the prophets, and *in* the psalms, concerning me."

The identification of Jesus as the Messiah deepens our understanding of the story of the Nativity, as well as of the preordained events that led to His Passion and death. Christians believe that although Jesus was the Messiah, His work is not yet done. For Christ will return, and His second coming will be the day of judgment, when sinners are punished and the righteous will live in God's kingdom forever after. Armed with this knowledge, let us now look more closely at Matthew and Luke's accounts of the Nativity.

Opposite: Because John the Baptist saluted Jesus with the words "Behold the Lamb of God, which taketh away the sin of the world" (John 1:29) when they encountered one another as adults, he is often portrayed with a lamb, as in this Hieronymus Bosch painting.

THE CONCEPTION AND BIRTH OF JOHN THE BAPTIST

Luke begins his gospel by relating the miraculous circumstances surrounding the conception and birth of John the Baptist, thereby heralding the ministry of Jesus, as also asserted by Mark: "As it is written in the prophets, Behold, I send my messenger before thy face, which shall prepare thy

way before ye." (Mark 1:2). Luke identifies John with Elias (Luke 1:17), the Greek form of the name of the prophet Elijah, who, according to Malachi 4:5, God will send "before the great and dreadful day of the LORD." It has been said that John is the link between the Old Testament and the New, and Luke makes it clear through the words of the angel Gabriel, God's messenger, that his miraculous conception and birth to an elderly couple was predestined. By decreeing that the baby should be called John, which means "God has favored" in Hebrew, rather than Zacharias, after his father, as would have been customary, Gabriel emphasized the special qualities that would enable John to fulfill his role as a prophet in preparing the way for Christ.

As an adult, "John did baptize in the wilderness, and preach the baptism of repentance and the remission of sins" (Mark 1:4), his baptism of Jesus in the River Jordan causing the Holy Spirit to descend upon Jesus, God to recognize him as his son, and his work to begin.

THE CONCEPTION OF JESUS AND THE ANNUNCIATION

Matthew tells us that Mary became pregnant with Jesus before she had "come together" with Joseph, a carpenter of Nazareth to whom she was betrothed, and that Joseph was therefore considering rejecting her until an angel appeared to him in a dream explaining that the father of her child

was the Holy Ghost. In Matthew 1:23, the angel repeats almost
verbatim the words of the prophet Isaiah, "Therefore the
Lord himself shall give you a sign; Behold, a virgin shall
conceive, and bear a son, and shall call his name Immanuel"
(Isaiah 7:14), Matthew adding that "Emmanuel" means "God
with us" (meaning, "God is among us in the world of men"),
thereby convincing Joseph to stand by Mary and go through
with the marriage.

Luke, by contrast, relates that the angel Gabriel made the Annunciation (the announcement of the incarnation of the son of God in human form) to Mary, rather than Joseph, at the same time informing her that her cousin Elisabeth, the future mother of John the Baptist, was six months pregnant. Mary rushed to visit her cousin, whereupon Elisabeth felt her baby leap in her womb for joy and addressed the younger Mary as "the mother of my Lord." Thanks to His parentage, Mary's unborn child was both the son of God and the "son of Man" referred to in Daniel 7:13–14 as the Messiah.

Right: *Luke (2:13–14) tells us that the shepherds witnessed "a multitude of the heavenly host praising God, and saying, Glory to God in the highest, and on earth peace, good will toward men" in celebration of Jesus' miraculous birth.*

Left: *Correggio's interpretation of the Nativity is inspired by Luke's gospel, in which we are told that Mary laid her newborn son in a humble manger because there was no room for them in the inn (Luke 2:7).*

THE NATIVITY

Both Matthew and Luke give Jesus' place of birth as Bethlehem, Luke taking pains to explain why Mary and Joseph had left Nazareth, where they were living, to go there, namely to comply with the Roman emperor's decree that his subjects should be taxed in their birthplaces. As Joseph was the head of the family, he and his wife duly traveled to Bethlehem, which, as a descendent of David (once a lowly shepherd of Bethlehem), was his hometown. Crucially, the birth of Jesus in Bethlehem fulfilled a prophecy made in Micah 5:2: "But thou, Bethlehem Ephratah, *though* thou be little among the thousands of Judah, *yet* out of thee shall he come forth unto me *that is* to be ruler in Israel."

The gospels' accounts of the Nativity otherwise differ, with only Luke telling us that Jesus was laid in a manger, there being no room available in teeming Bethlehem, and that an angel called shepherds in the vicinity to witness Jesus' manifestation on earth and glorify him.

And it is only from Matthew that we learn of the adoration of Jesus by the wise men, who had been alerted to the birth of the "King of the Jews" by the presence of "his star in the

Right: *By the mid-fifteenth century, when Gozzoli created this magnificent painting, the Magi were envisaged as being three wealthy and powerful kings rather than the unspecified number of "wise men" mentioned in Matthew's account.*

east." It is probable that the wise men, or Magi, were Chaldean, Persian, or Arabian astrologers who were skilled in the art of interpreting heavenly signs, and who, perhaps being familiar with Jewish Messianic belief, concluded that the star that had newly appeared in the night sky signaled the birth of the Messiah. In this way, Matthew underlines the significance of Jesus' birth to non-Jews, as well as to men whose wisdom commanded respect. Medieval tradition felt it apt to upgrade the Magi to kings, each representing one of the three continents that were known at that time, namely Europe, Africa, and Asia, thereby emphasizing the humility that these powerful men felt in the presence of the infant Jesus. Matthew does not specify the number of wise men, but the kings were later said to be three: Melchior, the giver of gold, Caspar, whose gift was frankincense, and Balthasar, who brought myrrh. Matthew does, however, list these gifts, no doubt on account of their symbolic and prophetic significance: gold denoting royalty; frankincense, or incense, the worship of God; and myrrh being a substance that was used to prepare bodies for burial, so that together these gifts signifed Jesus' kingship, divinity, mortality, and death.

THE PRESENTATION IN THE TEMPLE

According to Mosaic law (Leviticus 12), after giving birth to a male child, a Jewish woman is unclean for seven days (and her son must be circumcised when eight days old). Thirty-three days later, she must bring a lamb and pigeon or turtledove, or if a lamb is out of the question, two pigeons or turtledoves, to the temple for a priest to sacrifice and atone for her sins, whereupon she is cleansed. Luke confirms that Mary and Joseph abided by Mosaic law, combining her purification ritual with Jesus' presentation in the temple (in Jerusalem), as was customary for baby boys. There, Jesus was recognized and saluted as the Messiah by both Simeon (a devout old man whom the Holy Ghost had told would see the "Lord's Christ" before he died, "A light to lighten the Gentiles, and the glory of thy people Israel") and the prophetess Anna. Luke makes it clear that this was no ordinary baby!

Below: Bellini's painting depicts the moment when Simeon took the Christ child into his arms in the temple "and blessed God and said, Lord, now lettest thou thy servant depart in peace, according to thy word: For mine eyes have seen thy salvation" (Luke 2:28–30).

The Holy Family Leaves Bethlehem

Opposite: A Greek icon portraying Jesus as a grown man on the verge of fulfilling His destiny, the redemption of humankind through His suffering and cruel death.

As they searched for the baby that was "born King of the Jews," Matthew says that the wise men approached King Herod, hoping that he would know the child's whereabouts, thereby alerting the paranoid king to the birth of a potential challenger to his power, his concern being deepened by the chief priests' assertion that the Messiah would be born in Bethlehem. Although he accordingly sent the wise men to Bethlehem, and tried to trick them into returning to inform him of Jesus' location, they were warned of his evil purposes in a dream, and set off for their homeland without seeing Herod again. Matthew tells us that the enraged Herod tried to eliminate the infant's threat to his kingship by ordering that all children under two years of age in Bethlehem and thereabouts should be slaughtered. When this terrible precautionary measure had been carried out, Matthew goes on to say that the voice of Rachel, a mother figure of Israel who died in childbirth in Ramah, on the way to Bethlehem, could be heard lamenting the massacre.

Right: According to Matthew, an angel appeared to Joseph three times in a dream: firstly, to inform him that Mary had conceived a child by the Holy Ghost; secondly, to warn him to take his family and flee into Egypt to save their son's life; and thirdly, to tell him that it was safe to return home to Israel.

Having been alerted to Herod's deadly intent by an angel in a dream, Joseph had managed to spirit Mary and Jesus away to Egypt (thus fulfilling a prophecy that the son of God would come from Egypt) before the massacre began. Here, according to Matthew, they remained until Herod was dead. On hearing that Herod's son, Achelaus, had assumed the rulership of Judea, Joseph deemed it unsafe to venture to Bethlehem, and so it was that the Holy Family settled in Nazareth, in Galilee. Although Matthew's story of the wise men, Herod, and the Flight into Egypt are absent from Luke's account of the Nativity, Luke also confirms that they returned to Nazareth following Jesus' birth.

Right: Unlike deciduous trees, evergreens never shed their leaves, even when covered in a blanket of winter snow, which is why the Christmas tree is a potent symbol of immortality and of the resurrected Christ.

Left: *According to some traditions, Jesus' crown of thorns was fashioned from a sprig of holly, its red berries being said to represent the beads of blood drawn by its sharp leaves. In ancient times, red-berried holly was sacred to various Sun gods, while white-berried mistletoe was dedicated to goddesses of the Moon.*

CHRISTMAS

Throughout Advent (which starts on the first Sunday after November 30), Christians anticipate the anniversary of Christ's Nativity on December 25. It is a time when the words of the gospels ring out in the form of carols, Bible readings, and young actors' lines, even if these sometimes owe more to medieval additions and embellishments than to the New Testament. Christmastide traditionally ends on January 6, Twelfth Night, or the feast of the Epiphany (from the Greek *epiphaneia*, "an appearing"), which commemorates the manifestation of Christ to the Magi in the Western Church. Yet nowhere in the New Testament is it stated that the events of the Nativity occurred on these dates, so why are they celebrated then?

The answer has ancient roots that are grounded in Sun worship. The winter solstice, which can vary from year to year, but falls around December 22, heralds the weak winter Sun's increasing strength, which will reach its height at the summer solstice (around June 21). Pagan peoples consequently hailed the winter solstice as the occasion of the rebirth of the Sun god, whose decline, and eventual death, was believed to follow the autumnal equinox (on around September 23). The Romans, for example, saluted Sol Invictus, "the

Right: Giotto's beautiful portrayal of the First Christmas at Greccio, Italy, where St. Francis first recreated the Nativity scene (1223), beginning the traditional Christmas celebration that continues to this day.

unconquerable Sun," on December 25. Having found it impossible to eradicate the vestiges of such deep-rooted traditions, during the fourth century, the Christian Church simply imposed its own celebration, that of the Nativity, on its age-old predecessors. Similarly, the Christian Feast of the Annunciation, or Lady Day, which recalls the angel's appearance to Mary, falls on March 25, nine months before the supposed birth of Christ, but also around the date of the vernal equinox, one of the four great Sun festivals.

Right: The Holy Family—Jesus, Mary, and Joseph—as depicted by Raphael. The lamb that the infant Jesus is embracing represents his role as a sacrificial lamb whose innocent blood will wash away humankind's sins.

Jesus' Earthly Family

JESUS' FOREFATHERS

Previous page:
*Raphael envisaged
Mary and Joseph's
wedding ceremony as
taking place before a
magnificent temple.
Their marriage is
barely mentioned in
the gospels, however.*

1 The book of the generation of Jesus Christ, the son of David, the son of Abraham.

2 Abraham begat Isaac; and Isaac begat Jacob; and Jacob begat Judas and his brethren;

3 And Judas begat Phares and Zara of Thamar; and Phares begat Esrom; and Esrom begat Aram;

4 And Aram begat Aminadab; and Aminadab begat Naasson; and Naasson begat Salmon;

5 And Salmon begat Booz of Rachab; and Booz begat Obed of Ruth; and Obed begat Jesse;

6 And Jesse begat David the king; and David the king begat Solomon of her *that had been the wife of Urias;*

7 And Solomon begat Roboam; and Roboam begat Abia; and Abia begat Asa;

8 And Asa begat Josaphat; and Josaphat begat Joram; and Joram begat Ozias;

9 And Ozias begat Joatham; and Joatham begat Achaz; and Achaz begat Ezekias;

10 And Ezekias begat Manasses; and Manasses begat Amon; and Amon begat Josias;

11 And Josias begat Jechonias and his brethren, about the time they were carried away to Babylon:

12 And after they were brought to Babylon, Jechonias begat

Right: *Michelangelo's
lunettes of Jesus'
ancestors, as listed
by Matthew, in the
Sistine Chapel
include portrayals
of Jacob, whose son,
Joseph, married the
Virgin Mary.*

Salathiel; and Salathiel begat Zorobabel;

13 And Zorobabel begat Abiud; and Abiud begat Eliakim; and Eliakim begat Azor;

14 And Azor begat Sadoc; and Sadoc begat Achim; and Achim begat Eliud;

15 And Eliud begat Eleazar; and Eleazar begat Matthan; and Matthan begat Jacob;

16 And Jacob begat Joseph the husband of Mary, of whom was born Jesus, who is called Christ.

17 So all the generations from Abraham to David *are* fourteen generations; and from David until the carrying away into Babylon *are* fourteen generations; and from the carrying away into Babylon unto Christ *are* fourteen generations.

—MATTHEW 1:1–17

Above: This detail from a fresco by Giotto depicts the meeting at the Golden Gate of Joachim and Anna, who became the parents of the Virgin Mary.

JESUS' LINE OF DESCENT

23 And Jesus himself began to be about thirty years of age, being (as was supposed) the son of Joseph, which was *the son* of Heli,

24 Which was *the son* of Matthat, which was *the son* of Levi, which was *the son* of Melchi, which was *the son* of Janna, which was *the son* of Joseph,

25 Which was *the son* of Mattathias, which was *the son* of Amos, which was *the son* of Naum, which was *the son* of Esli, which was *the son* of Nagge,

26 Which was *the son* of Maath, which was *the son* of Mattathias, which was *the son* of Semei, which was *the son* of Joseph, which was *the son* of Juda,

27 Which was *the son* of Joanna, which was *the son* of Rhesa, which was *the son* of Zorobabel, which was *the son* of Salathiel, which was *the son* of Neri,

28 Which was *the son* of Melchi, which was *the son* of Addi, which was *the son* of Cosam, which was *the son* of Elmodam, which was *the son* of Er,

29 Which was *the son* of Jose, which was *the son* of Eliezer, which was *the son* of Jorim, which was *the son* of Matthat, which was *the son* of Levi,

Right: *An angel prevents Abraham from sacrificing his son, Isaac, in a dramatic scene from the brush of Caravaggio. According to Luke, both of these Jewish patriarchs were ancestors of Jesus.*

30 Which was *the son* of Simeon, which was *the son* of Juda, which was *the son* of Joseph, which was *the son* of Jonan, which was *the son* of Eliakim,

31 Which was *the son* of Melea, which was *the son* of Menan, which was *the son* of Mattatha, which was *the son* of Nathan, which was *the son* of David,

32 Which was *the son* of Jesse, which was *the son* of Obed, which was *the son* of Booz, which was *the son* of Salmon, which was *the son* of Naasson,

33 Which was *the son* of Aminadab, which was *the son* of Aram, which was *the son* of Esrom, which was *the son* of Phares, which was *the son* of Juda,

34 Which was *the son* of Jacob, which was *the son* of Isaac, which was *the son* of Abraham, which was *the son* of Thara, which was *the son* of Nachor,

35 Which was *the son* of Saruch, which was *the son* of Ragau, which was *the son* of Phalec, which was *the son* of Heber, which was *the son* of Sala,

36 Which was *the son* of Cainan, which was *the son* of Arphaxad, which was *the son* of Sem, which was *the son* of Noe, which was *the son* of Lamech,

37 Which was *the son* of Mathusala, which was *the son* of Enoch, which was *the son* of Jared, which was *the son* of Maleleel, which was *the son* of Cainan,

38 Which was *the son* of Enos, which was *the son* of Seth, which was *the son* of Adam, which was *the son* of God.

Above: *Titian's David and Goliath (1541). Both Matthew and Luke state that Jesus was descended from David, who was a giant-killing shepherd boy from Bethlehem before becoming king of Israel.*

—LUKE 3:23–38

JOSEPH'S DREAM

18 Now the birth of Jesus Christ was on this wise: When as his mother Mary was espoused to Joseph, before they came together, she was found with child of the Holy Ghost.

19 Then Joseph her husband, being a just *man* and not willing to make her a publick example, was minded to put her away privily.

20 But while he thought on these things, behold, the angel of the Lord appeared unto him in a dream, saying, Joseph, thou son of David, fear not to take unto thee Mary thy wife: for that which is conceived in her is of the Holy Ghost.

21 And she shall bring forth a son, and thou shalt call his name JESUS: for he shall save his people from their sins.

22 Now all this was done, that it might be fulfilled which was spoken of the Lord by the prophet, saying,

23 Behold, a virgin shall be with child, and shall bring forth a son, and they shall call his name Emmanuel, which being interpreted is, God with us.

24 Then Joseph being raised from sleep did as the angel of the Lord had bidden him, and took unto him his wife:

25 And knew her not till she had brought forth her firstborn son: and he called his name JESUS.

—MATTHEW 1:18–25

The Birth of John the Baptist

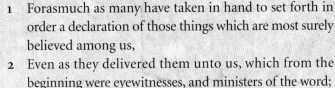

JOHN'S CONCEPTION

Previous page:
Andrea del Verrocchio's
portrayal of John the
Baptist baptizing Jesus
in the River Jordan.
According to Mark
(1:9–11), the Holy Spirit
descended upon Jesus
as He rose from the
water's surface.

Below: *Zacharias was*
terrified when an angel
appeared before him
(Luke 1:9–12).

1 Forasmuch as many have taken in hand to set forth in order a declaration of those things which are most surely believed among us,

2 Even as they delivered them unto us, which from the beginning were eyewitnesses, and ministers of the word;

3 It seemed good to me also, having had perfect understanding of all things from the very first, to write unto thee in order, most excellent Theophilus,

4 That thou mightest know the certainty of those things, wherein thou hast been instructed.

5 THERE was in the days of Herod, the king of Judaea, a certain priest named Zacharias, of the course of Abia: and his wife *was* of the daughters of Aaron, and her name *was* Elisabeth.

6 And they were both righteous before God, walking in all the commandments and ordinances of the Lord blameless.

7 And they had no child, because that Elisabeth was barren, and they both were *now* well stricken in years.

8 And it came to pass, that while he executed the priest's office before God in the order of his course,

9 According to the custom of the priest's office, his lot was to burn incense when he went into the temple of the Lord.

10 And the whole multitude of the people were praying without at the time of incense.

11 And there appeared unto him an angel of the Lord standing on the right side of the altar of incense.

12 And when Zacharias saw *him*, he was troubled, and fear fell upon him

13 But the angel said unto him, Fear not,

Zacharias: for thy prayer is heard; and thy wife Elisabeth shall bear thee a son, and thou shalt call his name John.

14 And thou shalt have joy and gladness; and many shall rejoice at his birth.

15 For he shall be great in the sight of the Lord, and shall drink neither wine nor strong drink; and he shall be filled with the Holy Ghost, even from his mother's womb.

16 And many of the children of Israel shall he turn to the Lord their God.

17 And he shall go before him in the spirit and power of Elias, to turn the hearts of the fathers to the children, and the disobedient to the wisdom of the just; to make ready a people prepared for the Lord.

18 And Zacharias said unto the angel, Whereby shall I know this? for I am an old man, and my wife well stricken in years.

19 And the angel answering said unto him, I am Gabriel, that stand in the presence of God; and am sent to speak unto thee, and to shew thee these glad tidings.

20 And, behold, thou shalt be dumb, and not able to speak, until the day that these things shall be performed, because thou believest not my words, which shall be fulfilled in their season.

21 And the people waited for Zacharias, and marvelled that he tarried so long in the temple.

22 And when he came out, he could not speak unto them: and they perceived that he had seen a vision in the temple: for he beckoned unto them, and remained speechless.

23 And it came to pass, that, as soon as the days of his ministration were accomplished, he departed to his own house.

24 And after those days his wife Elisabeth conceived, and hid herself five months, saying,

25 Thus hath the Lord dealt with me in the days wherein he looked on me, to take away my reproach among men.

—LUKE 1:1–25

Overleaf: *Fra Angelico's charming depiction of the moment when mothers-to-be Mary and Elisabeth (by then six months' pregnant) saluted one another following the Annunciation, as related by Luke (1:39–41).*

John's Birth

57 Now Elisabeth's full time came that she should be delivered; and she brought forth a son.

58 And her neighbours and her cousins heard how the Lord had shewed great mercy upon her; and they rejoiced with her.

59 And it came to pass, that on the eighth day they came to circumcise the child; and they called him Zacharias, after the name of his father.

60 And his mother answered and said, Not *so*; but he shall be called John.

61 And they said unto her, There is none of thy kindred that is called by this name.

62 And they made signs to his father, how he would have him called.

63 And he asked for a writing table, and wrote, saying, His name is John. And they marvelled all.

64 And his mouth was opened immediately, and his tongue *loosed*, and he spake, and praised God.

65 And fear came on all that dwelt round about them: and all these sayings were noised abroad throughout all the hill country of Judaea.

66 And all they that heard *them* laid *them* up in their hearts, saying, What manner of child shall this be! And the hand of the Lord was with him.

67 And his father Zacharias was filled with the Holy Ghost, and prophesied, saying,

68 Blessed *be* the Lord God of Israel; for he hath visited and redeemed his people,

69 And hath raised up an horn of salvation for us in the house of his servant David;

70 As he spake by the mouth of his holy prophets, which have been since the world began:

71 That we should be saved from our enemies, and from the hand of all that hate us;

72 To perform the mercy *promised* to our fathers, and to

remember his holy covenant;

73 The oath which he sware to our father Abraham,

74 That he would grant unto us, that we being delivered out of the hand of our enemies might serve him without fear,

75 In holiness and righteousness before him, all the days of our life.

76 And thou, child, shalt be called the prophet of the Highest: for thou shalt go before the face of the Lord to prepare his ways;

Page 42: John the Baptist, by Fra Angelico. The script on his banner reads ECCE AGNUS DEI, *the Latin for "Behold, the Lamb of God," the words with which he greeted Jesus.*

77 To give knowledge of salvation unto his people by the remission of their sins,

78 Through the tender mercy of our God; whereby the dayspring from on high hath visited us,

79 To give light to them that sit in darkness and *in* the shadow of death, to guide our feet into the way of peace.

80 And the child grew, and waxed strong in spirit, and was in the deserts till the day of his shewing unto Israel.

—LUKE 1:57–80

THE
ANNUNCIATION

Previous page:
According to Luke, Mary meekly accepted Gabriel's revelation of God's astonishing plans for her, saying, "Behold the handmaid of the Lord; be it unto me according to thy word" (Luke 1:38).

Right: *The angel Gabriel acts as God's messenger in both the Old and New Testament, and can therefore be seen as a bridge between Heaven and earth, the divine and humankind.*

THE ANGEL GABRIEL'S MESSAGE

26 And in the sixth month the angel Gabriel was sent from God unto a city of Galilee, named Nazareth,

27 To a virgin espoused to a man whose name was Joseph, of the house of David; and the virgin's name *was* Mary.

28 And the angel came in unto her, and said, Hail, *thou that art* highly favoured, the Lord *is* with thee: blessed *art* thou among women.

29 And when she saw *him*, she was troubled at his saying, and cast in her mind what manner of salutation this should be.

30 And the angel said unto her, Fear not, Mary: for thou hast found favour with God.

31 And, behold, thou shalt conceive in thy womb, and bring forth a son, and shalt call his name Jesus.

32 He shall be great, and shall be called the Son of the Highest: and the Lord God shall give unto him the throne of his father David:

33 And he shall reign over the house of Jacob for ever; and of his kingdom there shall be no end.

34 Then said Mary unto the angel, How shall this be, seeing I know not a man?

35 And the angel answered and said unto her, The Holy Ghost shall come upon thee, and the power of the Highest shall overshadow thee: therefore also that holy thing which shall be born of thee shall be called the Son of God.

36 And, behold, thy cousin Elisabeth, she hath also conceived a son in her old age: and this is the sixth month with her, who was called barren.

Left: *Many depictions of the Annunciation, including this one by Titian, show the angel Gabriel holding a white lily, a symbol of the Virgin Mary's purity.*

37 For with God nothing shall be impossible.

38 And Mary said, Behold the handmaid of the Lord; be it unto me according to thy word. And the angel departed from her.

39 And Mary arose in those days, and went into the hill country with haste, into a city of Juda;

40 And entered into the house of Zacharias, and saluted Elisabeth.

41 And it came to pass, that, when Elisabeth heard the salutation of Mary, the babe leaped in her womb; and Elisabeth was filled with the Holy Ghost:

42 And she spake out with a loud voice, and said, Blessed *art* thou among women, and blessed *is* the fruit of thy womb.

43 And whence *is* this to me, that the mother of my Lord should come to me?

44 For, lo, as soon as the voice of thy salutation sounded in mine ears, the babe leaped in my womb for joy.

45 And blessed *is* she that believed: for there shall be a performance of those things which were told her from the Lord.

46 And Mary said, My soul doth magnify the Lord,

47 And my spirit hath rejoiced in God my Saviour.

Below: Leonardo da Vinci vividly evokes the angel Gabriel's salutation of the Virgin Mary: "Hail, thou that art highly favoured, the Lord is with thee: blessed art thou among women" (Luke 1:28).

Left: *Fra Angelico's sensitive rendering of the Annunciation. Having informed Mary that she would "bring forth a son" (Luke 1:31), Gabriel went on to tell her that Elisabeth, her elderly cousin "who was called barren" (Luke 1:36), was also expecting a son.*

Below: During the Annunciation, as depicted below by Caravaggio, the angel Gabriel not only revealed her impending motherhood to the Virgin Mary, but also declared that "that holy thing which shall be born of thee shall be called the Son of God" (Luke 1:35).

48 For he hath regarded the low estate of his handmaiden: for, behold, from henceforth all generations shall call me blessed.

49 For he that is mighty hath done to me great things; and holy *is* his name.

50 And his mercy *is* on them that fear him from generation to generation.

51 He hath shewed strength with his arm; he hath scattered the proud in the imagination of their hearts.

52 He hath put down the mighty from *their* seats, and exalted them of low degree.

53 He hath filled the hungry with good things; and the rich he hath sent empty away.

54 He hath holpen his servant Israel, in remembrance of *his* mercy;

55 As he spake to our fathers, to Abraham, and to his seed for ever.

56 And Mary abode with her about three months, and returned to her own house.

—LUKE 1:26–56

The Nativity

THE SHEPHERDS

Previous page, opposite, and below: Luke's description of the shepherds' adoration of the swaddled Christ child as he lay in a manger (Luke 2:16) has inspired countless artists, including such masters as Caravaggio (previous page) and Hieronymus Bosch (opposite), as well as numerous children's-book illustrators (below).

1 And it came to pass in those days, that there went out a decree from Caesar Augustus, that all the world should be taxed.

2 (*And* this taxing was first made when Cyrenius was governor of Syria.)

3 And all went to be taxed, every one into his own city.

4 And Joseph also went up from Galilee, out of the city of Nazareth, into Judaea, unto the city of David, which is called Bethlehem; (because he was of the house and lineage of David:)

5 To be taxed with Mary his espoused wife, being great with child.

6 And so it was, that, while they were there, the days were accomplished that she should be delivered.

7 And she brought forth her firstborn son, and wrapped him in swaddling clothes, and laid him in a manger; because there was no room for them in the inn.

8 And there were in the same country shepherds abiding in the field, keeping watch over their flock by night.

9 And, lo, the angel of the Lord came upon them, and the glory of the Lord shone round about them: and they were sore afraid.

10 And the angel said unto them, Fear not: for, behold, I bring you good tidings of great joy, which shall be to all people.

11 For unto you is born this day in the city of David a Saviour, which is Christ the Lord.

12 And this *shall* be a sign unto you; Ye shall find the babe wrapped in swaddling clothes, lying in a manger.

Right: Luke tells us that the shepherds hurried to see the "Saviour, which is Christ our Lord" that the angel announced had just been born in the "city of David" (Luke 2:11). By depicting a shepherd holding a lamb, artist Lorenzo di Credi was emphasizing that the Christ child was the "Lamb of God" (John 1:29).

WHILE SHEPHERDS WATCHED

WHILE shepherds watch'd their flocks by night,
All seated on the ground,
The Angel of the LORD came down,
And glory shone around.

"Fear not," said he; for mighty dread
Had seized their troubled mind;
"Glad tidings of great joy I bring
To you and all mankind.

"To you in David's town this day
Is born of David's line
A Saviour, Who is CHRIST the LORD
And this shall be the sign:

"The heav'nly Babe you there shall find
To human view display'd,
All meanly wrapp'd in swathing bands,
And in a manger laid."

Thus spake the seraph; and forthwith
Appear'd a shining throng
Of Angels praising god, who thus
Address'd their joyful song:

"All glory be to GOD on high,
And to the earth be peace:
Good will henceforth from Heav'n to men
Begin and never cease."

13 And suddenly there was with the angel a multitude of the heavenly host praising God, and saying,

14 Glory to God in the highest, and on earth peace, good will toward men.

15 And it came to pass, as the angels were gone away from them into heaven, the shepherds said one to another, Let us now go even unto Bethlehem, and see this thing which is come to pass, which the Lord hath made known unto us.

16 And they came with haste, and found Mary, and Joseph, and the babe lying in a manger.

17 And when they had seen *it*, they made known abroad the saying which was told them concerning this child.

18 And all they that heard *it* wondered at those things which were told them by the shepherds.

19 But Mary kept all these things, and pondered *them* in her heart.

20 And the shepherds returned, glorifying and praising God for all the things that they had heard and seen, as it was told unto them.

—LUKE 2:1–20

Below: Matthew relates that the star that led the wise men to the baby Jesus "went before them, till it came and stood over where the young child was." (Matthew 2:9).

THE WISE MEN

Opposite and below:
All that Matthew tells us about the Magi is that they were "wise men from the east." Artists have depicted them in a wide variety of guises, from old men to powerful, wealthy kings.

1 Now when Jesus was born in Bethlehem of Judaea in the days of Herod the king, behold, there came wise men from the east to Jerusalem,

2 Saying, Where is he that is born King of the Jews? for we have seen his star in the east, and are come to worship him.

3 When Herod the king had heard *these things*, he was troubled, and all Jerusalem with him.

4 And when he had gathered all the chief priests and scribes of the people together, he demanded of them where Christ should be born.

5 And they said unto him, *in* Bethlehem of Judaea: for thus it is written by the prophet,

6 And thou Bethlehem, in the land of Juda, art not the least among the princes of Juda: for out of thee shall come a Governor, that shall rule my people Israel.

7 Then Herod, when he had privily called the wise men, enquired of them diligently what time the star appeared.

8 And he sent them to Bethlehem, and said, Go and search diligently for the young child; and when ye have found *him*, bring me word again, that I may come and worship him also.

9 When they had heard the king, they departed; and, lo, the star, which they saw in the east, went before them, till it came and stood over where the young child was.

10 When they saw the star, they rejoiced with exceeding great joy.

11 And when they were come into the house, they saw the young child with Mary his mother, and fell down, and worshipped him: and when they had opened their treasures, they presented unto him gifts; gold, and frankincense, and myrrh.

12 And being warned of God in a dream that they should not return to Herod, they departed into their own country another way.

—MATTHEW 2:1–12

Opposite: *One of the Magi kneels before the infant Christ in this fifteenth-century painting by Gentile da Fabriano.*

Below: *Velazquez chose to follow a medieval convention, namely depicting one of the wise men as an African king.*

Left: *According to Matthew, when the wise men "saw the young child with Mary his mother," they "fell down and worshipped him: and when they had opened their treasures, they presented unto him gifts; gold, and frankincense, and myrrh" (Matthew 2:11), a scene exquisitely rendered by Botticelli.*

WE THREE KINGS

We three Kings of Orient are:
Bearing gifts we traverse afar
Field and fountain, moor and mountain,
Following yonder star.
O star of wonder, star of night,
Star with royal beauty bright,
Westward leading, still proceeding,
Guide us to Thy perfect light.

Melchior:
Born a King on Bethlehem's plain,
Gold I bring to crown Him again,
King forever, ceasing never,
Over us all to reign.

Caspar:
Frankincense to offer have I,
Incense owns a Deity nigh,
Prayer and praising, all men raising,
Worship Him, God most High.

Balthazar:
Myrrh is mine, its bitter perfume
Breathes a life of gathering gloom:
Sorrowing, sighing, bleeding, dying,
Sealed in the stone-cold tomb.

Glorious now behold Him arise,
King and God and sacrifice,
Alleluia, alleluia;
Earth to the heavens replies.

Presented
at the Temple

SIMEON AND ANNA

Previous page and opposite: These images of the enthroned Madonna and Child are by the Italian artist Giovanni da Fiesole (c.1387–1455). Better known today as Fra Angelico ("the Angelic Brother"), da Fiesole was a Dominican friar whose piety is evident in his work.

21 And when eight days were accomplished for the circumcising of the child, his name was called JESUS, which was so named of the angel before he was conceived in the womb.

22 And when the days of her purification according to the law of Moses were accomplished, they brought *him* to Jerusalem, to present him to the Lord;

23 (As it is written in the law of the Lord, Every male that openeth the womb shall be called holy to the Lord;)

24 And to offer a sacrifice according to that which is said in the law of the Lord, A pair of turtledoves, or two young pigeons.

25 And, behold, there was a man in Jerusalem, whose name was Simeon; and the same man *was* just and devout, waiting for the consolation of Israel: and the Holy Ghost was upon him.

26 And it was revealed unto him by the Holy Ghost, that he should not see death, before he had seen the Lord's Christ.

27 And he came by the Spirit into the temple: and when the parents brought in the child Jesus, to do for him after the custom of the law,

28 Then took he him up in his arms, and blessed God, and said,

29 Lord, now lettest thou thy servant depart in peace, according to thy word:

30 For mine eyes have seen thy salvation,

31 Which thou hast prepared before the face of all people;

32 A light to lighten the Gentiles, and the glory of thy people Israel.

33 And Joseph and his mother marvelled at those things which were spoken of him.

34 And Simeon blessed them, and said unto Mary his mother, Behold, this *child* is set for the fall and rising again of many in Israel; and for a sign which shall be spoken against;

35 (Yea, a sword shall pierce through thy own soul also,) that the thoughts of many hearts may be revealed.

36 And there was one Anna, a prophetess, the daughter of Phanuel, of the tribe of Aser: she was of a great age, and had lived with an husband seven years from her virginity.

37 And she *was* a widow of about fourscore and four years,

Right: *Luke tells us that when Joseph and Mary (far left) brought Jesus to the temple "to present him to the Lord" (Luke 2:22), both Simeon and Anna (far right) hailed the infant as the Messiah.*

which departed not from the temple, but served *God* with fastings and prayers night and day.

38 And she coming in that instant gave thanks likewise unto the Lord, and spake of him to all them that looked for redemption in Jerusalem.

—LUKE 2:21–38

Below: *Giotto's Madonna is holding a white rose, a symbol of her virginity, or purity, as well as of her status as the "rose of heaven" of Christian tradition.*

ESCAPING TO SAFETY

THE FLIGHT INTO EGYPT

Previous page:
Joseph prioritized the safety of his wife and her child. Indeed, had it not been for Joseph, Jesus might have perished during Herod's Massacre of the Innocents.

Right: *Fra Angelico's vision of the Holy Family's Flight into Egypt, with Mary and Jesus riding to safety on a donkey and Joseph trudging along behind them.*

13 And when they [the wise men, or magi] were departed, behold, the angel of the Lord appeareth to Joseph in a dream, saying, Arise, and take the young child and his mother, and flee into Egypt, and be thou there until I bring thee word: for Herod will seek the young child to destroy him.

14 When he arose, he took the young child and his mother by night, and departed into Egypt:

15 And was there until the death of Herod: that it might be fulfilled which was spoken of the Lord by the prophet, saying, Out of Egypt have I called my son.

16 Then Herod, when he saw that he was mocked of the wise men, was exceeding wroth, and sent forth, and slew all the children that were in Bethlehem, and in all the coasts thereof, from two years old and

Right: *Matthew says that the Holy Family fled to Egypt "that it might be fulfilled which was spoken of the Lord by the prophet, saying, Out of Egypt have I called my son" (Matthew 2:15). The prophet to whom Matthew is referring is Hosea (see Hosea 11:1).*

Opposite: *Raphael's portrayal of the Madonna and Child.*

Below: *Caravaggio's interpretation of the rest stop that the Holy Family were said to have taken on the way.*

under, according to the time which he had diligently inquired of the wise men.

17 Then was fulfilled that which was spoken by Jeremy the prophet, saying,

18 In Rama was there a voice heard, lamentation, and weeping, and great mourning, Rachel weeping *for* her children, and would not be comforted, because they are not.

—MATTHEW 2:13–18

THE RETURN OF THE HOLY FAMILY TO NAZARETH

19 But when Herod was dead, behold, an angel of the Lord appeareth in a dream to Joseph in Egypt,

20 Saying, Arise, and take the young child and his mother, and go into the land of Israel: for they are dead which sought the young child's life.

21 And he arose, and took the young child and his mother, and came into the land of Israel.

22 But when he heard that Archelaus did reign in Judaea in the room of his father Herod, he was afraid to go thither: notwithstanding, being warned of God in a dream, he turned aside into the parts of Galilee:

23 And he came and dwelt in a city called Nazareth: that it might be fulfilled which was spoken by the prophets, He shall be called a Nazarene.

—MATTHEW 2:19–23

39 And when they had performed all things according to the law of the Lord, they returned into Galilee, to their own city Nazareth.

40 And the child grew, and waxed strong in spirit, filled with wisdom: and the grace of God was upon him.

—LUKE 2:39–40

Opposite: "And Mary said, My soul doth magnify the Lord, And my spirit hath rejoiced in God my Saviour. For he hath regarded the low estate of his handmaiden: for, behold, from henceforth all generations shall call me blessed" (Luke 1:46–48).

INDEX